The New Bullying

M000015198

How social media, social exclusion, laws and suicide have changed our definition of bullying – and what to do about it

Michigan State University

School of Journalism

Read The Spirit Books

an imprint of
David Crumm Media, LLC
Canton, Michigan

For more information and further discussion, visit

http://news.jrn.msu.edu/bullying/

Published By
Read The Spirit Books
an imprint of
David Crumm Media, LLC
42015 Ford Rd., Suite 234
Canton, Michigan, USA

For information about customized editions, bulk purchases or permissions, contact David Crumm Media, LLC at info@David-CrummMedia.com

Contents

Acknowledgements

WE TOOK ON THE task of creating and publishing a book in 100 days because, just a few miles from our campus, the Michigan Legislature passed a law that gave school districts six months to create or review their anti-bullying policies.

Those policies were to grow out of community conversations. We thought that, besides covering the conversations, journalists could contribute to them with projects like this.

We had a lot of help.

We first want to thank Kevin and Tammy Epling, the parents of Matt Epling, after whom Michigan's anti-bullying law is named. The signing of that bill was a milestone in their journey and the impetus for our work. Their busy speaking schedule meant they had to move up a planned visit with us and we met them in our fourth class. They explained how bullying has changed in the past 15 years and how this has created a disconnect between adults and students. They gave our work direction and their ideas suggested the title for this project: *The New Bullying*.

Glenn Stutzky, a clinical instructor in the Michigan State University School of Social Work, has spent his career examining cycles of aggression. He generously came to talk with us and heard our story ideas, suggesting sources and new angles. If you learn anything from this book, it is because he was one of our teachers.

Two state senators contributed mightily to our understanding of the causes of bullying, the obstacles to legislating against it and the ways bullying laws are changing. They are Republican Sen. Rick Jones and Democratic Sen. Gretchen Whitmer.

Cooley School of Law professor Patrick Corbett is a former federal prosecutor and assistant U.S. attorney. He spoke about how social media and the Patriot Act have changed the circumstances and criminality of cyberbullying and how bullying is now seen by some as a civil rights issue. He also invited us to attend a meeting of the Washtenaw County Cyber Citizenship Coalition.

Retired Washtenaw County Sheriff's Department Sgt. Carl Werner gave us his perspective as a law enforcement officer who has worked in schools and with domestic violence.

We also are in debt to the MSU chapter of Phi Sigma Pi, which invited us to attend and appear on a campus panel about bullying.

Stutzky, who immerses himself in research, told us that the journalist's contribution to public discourse is to put a human face on the numbers. We had help with that, from many sources, especially Unis Middle School in Dearborn, whose students talked on camera about their bullying experiences.

We hope we have accurately conveyed the bullying story and the perspectives of the people who explained it.

Credits

Cover Design

Cover design by **Leslie Tilson**.

Cover illustration photos licensed from iStockphoto by Jani Bryson, Paul Morton, Cindy Singleton, Stacy Able, Jani Bryson and Juanmonino.

Authors, editors and contributors

Dmitri Barvinok is in the class of 2013, studying journalism. He is specializing in environmental reporting.

Seth Beifel is in the class of 2012, studying journalism and international relations. He is from Philadelphia and has never written a book before, and said this has been an interesting experience, to say the least.

Hayley Beitman is in the class of 2012, studying journalism with a specialization in design and photography. She is a contributing writer and photographer at The Odyssey at Michigan State.

Lynn Bentley is in the class of 2012, studying journalism.

Colby Berthume is in the class of 2012, studying journalism. He is specializing in public relations. He is currently working at a non-profit organization that offers job training for people with disabilities.

J.T. Bohland is in the class of 2012, studying journalism with a specialization in broadcasting. He has written for The Clarkston News and is an entertainment writer at Revue Magazine in Lansing.

Tony Briscoe is in the class 2012, majoring in journalism with a specialization in public affairs reporting. He has written for The Detroit News, Automotive News, and B.L.A.C. Detroit Magazine, among others.

Tommy Franz is a political science and sports journalism student in the class of 2012. After graduation, he will attend Marquette law school to study sports and entertainment law.

Rachel Jackson is in the class of 2013, studying journalism. She hopes to either become a politics and government reporter in Washington, D.C., or a war correspondent.

Alethia Kasben is in the class of 2012, studying journalism and public relations. She hopes to attend law school and pursue a career in politics.

Devyne Lloyd is in the class of 2013, studying journalism. She aspires to be a food critic.

Allen Martin is in the class of 2012, studying journalism with a concentration in sports broadcasting. He has interned at WLNS TV News, the Big Ten Network, and as a news/sports reporter at HOMTV in Haslett, Mich.

Dustin Petty is in the class of 2012, studying journalism. He hopes to one day operate a non-profit for LGBTQ youth.

Nicholas Roddy is in the class of 2012, studying journalism and international relations. He works as a student director for the Big Ten Network and wants to work in sports production.

Samantha Schmitt is in the class of 2012, studying journalism and public relations. She hopes to work in sports.

Leslie Tilson is in the class of 2013, studying journalism and political science. After graduation, she hopes to attend law school.

Lynne Werner is in the class of 2013, studying journalism. She hopes to one day work for a music magazine.

Publisher **John Hile** is co-founder and publisher at David Crumm Media, LLC. He is co-founder and a board member at Hilgraeve, Inc., a leader in communications software and services.

Editor **Joe Grimm** is a visiting editor in residence at the MSU School of Journalism. He spent more than 30 years in newspaper newsrooms and more than 40 years working with students. He has worked on about 10 books.

Preface

BULLYING IS AS OLD as Cain and Abel, one middle-school teacher said. A retired high school administrator called bullying "the flavor of the month." A journalism professor questioned whether, in 2012, there was much new to say about bullying since a project on the subject had been published 15 years earlier.

Yes, there is something new. The past 15 years have been a turning point in bullying.

In 1999 at Columbine High School near Denver, two students killed 13 people and themselves in a stunning spree of school violence. Within four months, Georgia passed the first school anti-bullying law in the nation.

In 2001, the book "Bullycide: Death at Playtime" coined a new word for people who take their own lives after being bullied. Canadian educator Bill Belsey is credited with coining the word cyberbullying that same year.

In 2001, in response to the Sept. 11 terror attacks of that year, the Patriot Act criminalized the use of computers to threaten security. Those laws have been used in bullying cases.

In 2003, MySpace was founded.

In 2004, Facebook was launched.

In 2005, the video-sharing site YouTube was created.

In 2006, Twitter began.

In 2010, Georgia updated and expanded that first anti-bullying law.

In 2011, the White House and the U.S. Departments of Education and Health and Human Services held a national conference on bullying.

Laws, technology and taboos have changed in important ways over the past 15 years. These developments have changed bullying forever.

The bullying that happened 50 or even 20 years ago is not the bullying we see today. Some examples:

- More frequently, student suicides are linked to bullying. Although hard to track, anecdotal evidence and greater publicity indicate the number is rising.
- The first generation to grow up with constant mobile and social media can send and receive bullying messages 24 hours a day, wherever they are. Cyberbullying is widespread, it is real and has had tragic consequences.
- It has become OK to talk about bullying openly. Schools that whispered about bullying to protect their image now hold rallies opposing it. News media are more open about teen suicide, too.
- Students now produce anti-bullying messages that are seen by hundreds of thousands.
- News about bullying and support for its victims is exchanged globally.
- Internet searches for bullying information are up markedly.
- Bullying has become an open issue in business, legal and governmental offices.

The past 15 years have clearly changed bullying. Yet, a generational disconnect persists between today's adults who were bullied as kids and today's students who are experiencing a new kind of bullying.

At Michigan State University, an advanced journalism class reported on the new bullying and created a website and this book.

Kevin and Tammy Epling, whose son Matt, 14, took his own life after being bullied, helped us understand that we can contribute to the discussion by describing the new bullying.

PART 1
What is bullying?

CHAPTER 1

Our starting point: How do we define bullying?

THE NATIONAL DEBATE ABOUT bullying starts with a simple question: What is it?

Like many organizations, schools and legislatures across the country, the Obama administration tried to come up with a definition at the White House Conference on Bullying Prevention in March 2011.

Kevin Epling, who lost his son Matt to suicide after being bullied by older students, was part of the panel asked to devise a definition. Epling remembered sitting in a White House office for hours because no one could agree on one definition.

"The funny thing is that with all of the discussion of the definition," said Epling, "there was not consensus. There are several definitions available. I tried to cut out the fluff and get to the heart of why people bully - not how they bully."

What the White House conference finally settled on is a laundry list of what constitutes bullying and what doesn't, where bullying takes place and what types of bullying exist. Essentially,

Kevin Epling is the founder and co-director of Bully Police USA

as reported on the website StopBullying.gov, bullying must be aggressive, repetitive and include an imbalance of power.

This definition is the same that was adopted in 2008 by the National Parent-Teacher Association, a non-profit collaboration of educators and parents, citing the U.S. Department of Health and Human Services.

On the other hand, the National Education Association, a union representing more than 3.2 million educators, relied on the targets of bullying for a definition.

It used a study that asked elementary school students what they thought bullying was. Their thoughts became the definition put forward for teachers across the nation:

> Bullying is defined as the use of one's strength or popularity to injure, threaten, or embarrass another person. Bullying can be physical, verbal, or social. It is not bullying when two students of about the same strength argue or fight.

Organizations that work to serve students aren't the only ones trying to define bullying.

As of March 2012, each state – with the exception of Montana – has adopted some measure of anti-bullying legislation, meaning that each state has its own definition.

In 1999, Georgia became the first state to adopt anti-bullying legislation. Twelve years later, however, after a bullied student committed suicide, Georgia State Rep. Mike Jacobs said the law didn't go far enough because it didn't apply to elementary schools and only defined bullying as physical harassment.

In 2011, the state passed a new anti-bullying law with a new, broadened definition. The new law required the Georgia Department of Education to give more specific guidelines to school districts on what constitutes bullying and how to deal with it.

The definition expanded to include any single "intentional written, verbal, or physical act, which a reasonable person would perceive as being intended to threaten, harass, or intimidate." The new law did not stop at repetitive physical acts.

The new law also recognized changes in the impact that computers and the Internet have on bullying. The revised bill counts bullying as "an act which occurs . . . by use of data or software that is accessed through a computer, computer systems, computer network, or other electronic technology of a local school system."

It's becoming evident to lawmakers and parents alike that bullying has changed, yet still cannot be easily defined.

— *Dustin Petty*

CHAPTER 2

The unseen bullying of social exclusion

BULLYING HAS TAKEN A new form on playgrounds across the country. Instead of children being teased, pushed around or called names, they are shunned and not invited to join games and activities.

Children are being socially excluded.

According to Dr. Lynn Todman, the term "social exclusion" was initially used during the 1970s by a French politician trying to describe those excluded from the labor market. Todman, executive director of the Institute on Social Exclusion at Adler School of Professional Psychology in Chicago, studies the subject in terms of socioeconomics.

"Social exclusion is actively created by the structures and systems that organize and guide the functioning of our society," said Todman. "These structures and systems determine the allocation of rights, resources and opportunities such as food, safety, education, health, due process and shelter."

While Todman's studies focus on social exclusion in underserved populations, she is quick to point out that the result is the same in groups.

"There is research . . . showing that when people feel like they're being excluded, they lose their willingness to self-regulate," said Todman.

Dr. Edyth Wheeler of Towson University in Baltimore County, Md., agrees and has studied social exclusion of children and young adults.

"Four-year-olds are masters at this," she said. "When they say 'I'm not going to be your friend anymore,' they are making the threat of exclusion. Children at that age are at the point where their need for adult approval is declining and they are dependent on peer approval."

Wheeler said she doesn't believe that children learn from their parents or other adults how to exclude others. Instead, she believes it is a knowledge of the human condition which leads to the ability – and desire – to exclude peers.

"It's this innate understanding that makes people want to be accepted and let in," she said. "To show we have power, we cannot accept them and leave them out. Or to cement ourselves as a group – to be a stronger 'we' – we'll identify a 'them.'"

According to her work, young girls are specifically good at performing acts of social exclusion. For them, it's a strong and powerful tool used to negotiate their world and relationships.

There is good news, according to Wheeler, if you're the victim of social exclusion.

"It's not a permanent condition," she said. "It peaks and then goes away. Part of it is about finding your own identity."

Teachers and parents may also play a role in preventing social exclusion or healing the hurt.

"Adults really need to listen to their children and to pick up the signals," said Wheeler. "Children need to trust that somebody can help them. If the message can be that everyone is valued and everyone will be listened to, the situations can become better.

She added, "In classrooms, teachers can create a sense of community and be very aware of grouping. Really, it all goes back to the responsibility of the adult."

— *Dustin Petty*

CHAPTER 3

The case for legislation

IF LOCKERS AND LINOLEUM tiles could talk, they would tell an unpleasant tale of students around the United States.

Concern about bullying is growing and a major research group indicates that 28 percent of all students between 12 and 18 are victims of maltreatment.

More than 47 percent of bullied students reported they have been victimized specifically in school hallways and stairwells, according to the U.S Department of Education's National Center for Education statistics.

Another nine percent of victims said they were bullied in the bathroom or locker room and another six percent are harassed on the school bus.

This comes as no surprise to high school teacher Carman Smith. An English teacher at Wylie E. Groves High School in Beverly Hills, Mich., Smith said he intervenes in bullying altercations at least once a day.

"A lot of times it happens in between classes in the hallways, it happens in the locker rooms, it happens in common areas, before school, after schools, on the bus, at the bus stop . . . I would say most happen outside of the classroom."

While many students reported being bullied in transition, 33 percent of victims identified the classroom as a bullying focal point.

Smith said teachers at his school are more than capable of handling bullying in the classroom. The school, roughly 1,400 students, has anti-bullying policies as well as prevention programs such as peer mediation. The district also has had seminars where teachers undergo training on how to resolve bullying situations.

"It is a part of our house rules that we report any type of hazing or bullying or someone being treated unfairly," said Smith. "Each individual case is handled separately, so the actual consequences depend on the situation."

One of the biggest problems the group is struggling to manage now is cyberbullying. According to a 2011 Pew Internet report, eight percent of students have been bullied online in the last 12 months. Smith, who's been teaching since 2002, said bullying has become an unmanageable problem because online confrontations spill into the classroom.

Today, 82 percent of children have an online presence before they turn two, according to a recent study by AVG, an Internet security company, so maintaining a safe web of social networks is important.

"I think bullying has always been there, but it's gotten worse because of cyberbullying," said Smith. "It's brought on a whole new phenomenon. The access these kids have to the Web, and what they can do with the Web, it's brought bullying to a whole new level."

Because bullying has gone beyond the schoolyard, Smith says it's up to parents to monitor their children's activity. He encourages parents to create their own social media pages to supervise their kids. "I think more parental control of these social media sites could help the problem. I have no business going on a student's Facebook or Twitter page. There's only so much I can do in the (school) hours."

Michigan Sen. Rick Jones gets up at 5:30 a.m. every day to meet constituents in a coffee shop, but it was in his office where the mother of a cyberbullying victim showed him messages on her daughter's Facebook profile that made the girl afraid to go to school.

The messages were horrible, said Jones, a sponsor of Matt's Safe School Law.

Matt's Safe School Law was signed on Dec. 6, 2011, and required every school district in the state to draft an anti-bullying policy within six months. The law required policies to be submitted to the State Board of Education for review.

The law came to fruition largely with the help of Matt's father, Kevin Epling, who wanted to save families from experiencing the same loss he and his wife, Tammy, suffered. In 2002, Matt took his life after he was bullied by older students.

Kevin Epling talked about some of the ways bullying has changed in recent years. Photo by Hayley Beitman.

Forty-nine states now have anti-bullying laws, leaving just Montana. One reason for the increased pressure on anti-bullying legislation is because the federal government and various political organizations are now labeling bullying as a crime.

Jones is now looking at drafting cyber-bullying legislation.

This potential legislation, however, runs into First Amendment issues, he said, since freedom of speech permits people to express themselves online.

"I think it goes beyond freedom of speech," Jones said, referring back to the hurtful Facebook messages.

According to the National Conference of State Legislators, all 50 states have laws to combat cyberstalking, cyberharrasment, and cyberbullying, but not every state has protections against each. For example, Michigan has no explicit law against cyberbullying.

Cyberbullying is defined as cyberharrasment that takes place in school or targets minors.

Patrick Corbett, a professor of criminal law at Cooley Law School, says that teens are often unaware that they're breaking the law when they bully on Facebook.

In fact, when shown threatening text messages, many high school students are unfazed, Corbett said, believing that to be fairly normal communication.

For example, there are already laws that prohibit a person from posting messages, true or false, on social networks or through text messaging, if their intent is to harass another individual.

Another trend in high schools is creating a fake Facebook account to post embarrassing information, photos or messages. In some states, this is identity theft, and if the postings cause two or more people to contact the victimized student, a second charge is added, one that is punishable by a maximum of two years in prison.

"I question whether or not new statutes are needed," Corbett said.

Juvenile cases are not prosecuted often, potentially leading the public to believe that these kinds of offenses go unpunished.

"Anecdotally, I think a lot of these are being handled in the school," Corbett said.

If cyberstalking and online harassment incidents continue to rise, and if media coverage continues to cover resulting tragedies, prosecutors may begin bringing more and more juveniles to court, to set an example and dissuade other teens. In some places around the country, this has already begun.

Recent cases in Florida and Illinois have brought the issue to national attention by taking teenagers to court. In Florida, two teenagers were charged with aggravated stalking of a minor after creating a fake Facebook page for their victim and using it to post inappropriate comments and photos. Similarly, in Illinois, a mother sued after her son was identified as gay on a fake Facebook profile.

On Aug. 12, 2010, Associate Attorney General Tom Perrelli spoke at the Department of Education's Bullying Summit in Washington, D.C. He stressed how the prevention of bullying falls not only on the shoulders of teachers and administrators, but also law enforcement and the federal government. In his speech, he introduced a new anti-bullying initiative through the Department of

Justice. The Office of Juvenile Justice and Delinquency Prevention "is developing a five-bulletin series on the topic of peer victimization in schools based on three studies funded by OJJDP and conducted by the National Center for School Engagement," Perrelli said in his speech.

In the first bulletin of the series, released in December 2011, the authors pointed out that bullying is a complex social and emotional phenomenon that impacts victims in many ways. However, in the entire bulletin, there is no mention of any statistics on the prevalence of bullying in America.

One of the most thorough studies on the statistics of bullying in American schools was conducted by the National Center for Education Statistics in 2009. The study surveyed more than 25 million students between the ages of 12 and 18 for the 2008-2009 school year. The study showed that over 7 million students, or 28 percent of those studied, were bullied at school. The most common form of bullying was being called names or insulted. Other forms of bullying involved physical harm, social exclusion, and destruction of property.

According to the OJJDP's website, the most common school crime in America is theft. The OJJDP found that about 20% of students were involved in theft crimes.

The disparity between these two statistics shows the Department of Justice does not view bullying as a crime because, according to the Department, the most common school crime is theft. As the state governments are moving forward with anti-bullying policy, the federal government is lagging behind.

— *Tony Briscoe, Nicholas Roddy and Dmitri Barvinok*

CHAPTER 4

Change of schools can make the new kids vulnerable

MOST PEOPLE ARE FAMILIAR with classic first-day-of-school movie scenes where freshmen carry seniors' books, do their chores or get pushed around.

The transition from middle school to high school, or even elementary to middle school, can be difficult, already filled with changes and uncomfortable situations. The American Civil Liberties Union has worked to eliminate racial and gender hazing, and protect children who are most vulnerable, but there is still a lot of work to be done.

An 8th grade history teacher at a private middle school in Bloomfield Hills, Mich., shared his views on the transition to high school and how the pressure to fit in is a factor. He said that bullying is a problem in all types of schools, in all grades, in all social groups.

He said the major reason for bullying is that kids go from being "top dog" at their old school to the bottom of the social ladder at their new school.

"They often do or say things that they normally wouldn't do, or say, just to fit in. Middle school is all about fitting in. As much as the parents want their children to be pushing themselves academically, the main priority for many middlers is to fit in," he said.

"The social peer pressure is really intense and can get normal, nice kids to do some really cruel stuff for a cheap laugh or acceptance into a 'cooler' group. I can think of hundreds of examples of this happening. Sometimes it's innocent, and sometimes the situations leave lasting scars. Fortunately, we haven't had the cases of suicide as a result of bullying here, but it's a genuine fear that we have around here."

He said strategies for preventing this include closer monitoring by teachers and for smaller group activities like advisory groups and homeroom. "In tight-knit communities like ours, and this is probably true in many private schools where the class sizes are small and the parents are really involved, kids don't have as many opportunities to be sneaky and to do things without being caught. Also, because of programs like advisory and having counselors on staff, students typically have someone that they can talk to about the bullying and it can get squashed before it gets out of control."

He attended a public school where classes where huge, teachers were distant and counselors were overwhelmed with more serious cases in which bullying had escalated. He found that often, the quieter bullying is harder to control in private schools. "I think it often flies under the radar here a bit because it often isn't the blatant in-your-face type of bullying that you see in other schools."

Social media bullying and cyberbullying are very hard to monitor and discourage, he said. "We see that here quite a bit, someone writing something about someone else on Facebook or Twitter or other places like that. Kids creating 'I hate BLANK' pages and getting people to 'like' it."

Teachers who are computer savvy themselves say that middle schoolers have gotten way too advanced and smart with the new technology. "You just can't patrol it. It's something that schools try to monitor, but almost always fail miserably." Education, he said, can really help students understand the consequences of their actions. "We try to educate the students on the impacts of social and cyberbullying and try to get them to understand the lasting pain they can cause and the paper trail that they can often accumulate because nothing is ever really deleted from cyberspace."

"As far as what I was taught in college about bullying, well, it wasn't a whole lot." The problem is that many teachers were in school more than 15 years ago before bullying was a buzzword. "My education classes sort of glossed over the issue. We were taught to take advantage of 'teachable' moments, but to be very careful not to get too involved in some of the personal issues that students sometimes wanted to open up about."

He said that now that bullying is so hot, it is a topic at every educational conference and is part of lots of in-service and professional development around the country. His friends who teach in Vermont, New Hampshire and Ohio often talk about how their schools are trying to crack down on bullying.

As a teacher, he feels that unless it is very blatant and in the halls or classroom, it is extremely hard for teachers to identify bullying or to do anything about it.

He said that sometimes it's a group of kids giving another student the cold shoulder or just shutting them out of their normal social circle, which is very hard to reprimand. He doesn't see bullying getting worse but he has seen it change over his years as a teacher.

"It's tough to watch, but you just have to try to talk to the individual being shut out and remind them that it really isn't the end of the world and that in a couple of years . . . maybe even months or weeks, this dynamic will change and to remember what this feels like and to never be a part of a group that does this to someone else."

— *Hayley Beitman*

CHAPTER 5

Private schools can help, but have their issues too

FORTY-NINE STATES NOW HAVE anti-bullying laws, and most require public school districts to have anti-bullying policies. Bullying does not happen only at public schools.

However, there are more than 33,000 private schools in the United States with about 5.5 million students in attendance. State laws do not cover private schools. It is up to private school administrations to create and enforce policies on bullying.

Parents now send their children to private schools to avoid bullying, according to OurKids.net. At private schools, there are generally more teachers per student and that could lead to a higher probability of bullying being detected. Private schools also have more resources and programs to help students stay out of trouble. Studies by the National Center for Education Statistics show that bullying is less prevalent in private schools than in public schools.

Private schools are not immune to bullying, though. In 2011, an eighth grader was told to "man up" by her advisor when she was harassed at the Seattle Girls' School. The girl was frequently called names and the bullies even started having meetings in the bathroom to talk about her while she was in the bathroom stall. The bullying caused the girl to leave the school, and the girl's parents sued.

The girl said that each grade singled out a different girl every year to bully. In a Seattle Post Intelligencer article about the situation, the girl's mother said that the school tolerated the bullies because it did not want to jeopardize funding from their parents.

The school was started in 2000 with a Bill & Melinda Gates Foundation grant and tuition was about $15,000.

The Seattle Girls' School is a member of the National Association of Independent Schools, an association aimed at being the national voice of independent schools. Patrick Bassett, President of the NAIS, said that they "are very serious about (bullying) because it is so damaging."

In a phone interview, he said "most of our schools have an anti-bullying curriculum just like they have an anti-racism curriculum."

As far as whose responsibility it is to stop bullying, Bassett said it is up to the students, teachers and parents.

Patrick Bassett, NAIS president.

"Adults have to be conscious and intervene quickly and dramatically, but by the time a kid becomes a bully, there is already something else going on in his life," he said.

Independent schools are effective in combating bullying, Bassett said, because of the "contractual relationship the schools have with the kids and parents that says they have to be good citizens both inside and outside of school. If there is bullying outside of school, it is still under the jurisdiction of the school."

— *Nicholas Roddy*

CHAPTER 6

Teachers wish for more training, attention on the issue

ALTHOUGH MANY SCHOOLS ALREADY have anti-bullying policies, many teachers find themselves searching for more effective ways to combat bullying in their classrooms.

Laws alone are not enough, some teachers say, and training would help.

Most states have school bullying policies and are adding policies against cyberbullying and hazing, but many teachers wonder how effective laws can be.

"I think that Pennsylvania's anti-bullying laws in schools are somewhat effective, although I wish it was more straightforward and gave the consequences of certain actions so each school is on the same page," said Lauren Sady, a first, second and third grade teacher in the Philadelphia School District. She said complicated definitions of bullying can be a problem.

"The law creates more obstacles for the administration because bullying is bullying and there should not have to be a long list of criteria to go through before a child faces consequences. This may allow for more time for the student to think that he /she did no wrong, or come up with more ways to bully other children."

Although anti-bullying laws may create some hurdles for schools, they do give the school administration some legal ground to stand on.

Steve Hudock, a sixth, seventh and eighth grade teacher in Michigan's Van Buren Public School system, said, "Well, I would have to say that I do not feel that it (the law) has had a significant impact on things. Students still get picked on and we still sort things out.

"I think that the law is important in that it gives the school something to back up the decisions and discipline actions taken against students who bully or harass others. I do not feel it has an impact on students' actions toward one another."

As relationships are carried on in more digital ways, it is increasingly important for teachers and students alike to learn effective ways of dealing with bullying.

Sady said, "There was nothing specific that I learned while getting my teaching certificate that dealt with bullying, but I wish there was. I am learning more and more each day, ways to deal with different types of bullying in my classroom."

Bullying is occurring earlier and earlier in children's lives and it is leading to more behaviors that children should not be exhibiting at all, let alone at such a young age.

Students are also afraid to tell adults about bullying because they are afraid to get in trouble, so they keep the issue to themselves, which may or may not lead to a bigger issue.

Often, teachers have to rely on the administration to deal with bullying problems in their classroom, because the gravity of the situation is beyond the reach of good classroom management.

"In a bullying situation, we were taught to have a zero-tolerance policy," said Elizabeth Nork, a chemistry education student at Purdue University. "We are supposed to immediately put a stop to any bullying and send the student to the office and let the administration deal with the issue. We talked about having a zero-tolerance policy but never went into depth as to what that means. It would be nice to dedicate more time talking about the bullying issue in schools, because I really don't feel all that prepared to deal with it going into my student teaching."

Preparation is key when it comes to dealing with issues and more school districts are supplementing teacher training with information on bullying. But the question remains: are teachers well enough prepared to deal with issues of severe bullying, or noticing the signs early enough to take action before bullying turns into something bigger?

Hudock said, "I have to say that, other than making staff aware of bullying issues, I really don't feel that there has been much effort made to help staff address the issues. I have personally subscribed to a publication called 'Teaching Tolerance' which has provided me with articles and materials to read and use in the classroom. But, I feel that these are things that are shared with us as a situation arises. I do not feel that any planned efforts have been made to prepare staff to deal with bullying in schools or the new law."

Hudock said that it is very hard to implement a successful set of guidelines and policies unless there is district level support for the building level decisions, and without it the changes will not be effective.

— *Leslie Tilson*

CHAPTER 7

Timeline

FORTY-NINE STATES HAVE BULLYING legislation on the books. This timeline shows when each state signed their bills into law.

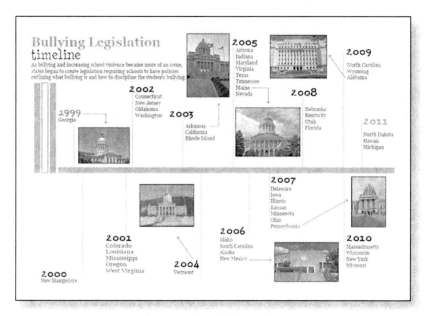

Illustration by Alethia Kasben.

CHAPTER 8

Bullying by boys tends to be more physical and visible

THE BEHAVIORS OF BOYS and girls who bully can be similar, but spotting bullying among boys is much easier than it is with girls.

David P. Farrington, professor of psychological criminology at Cambridge University, wrote that boys who bully are more physical than girls.

Psychiatrist Ann Ruth Turkel wrote that boys are more physical because of the way they are raised. Boys are encouraged to kick their negative feelings away, while girls are taught to avoid direct confrontation.

She also wrote that boys usually bully strangers or acquaintances, while girls bully within their group of friends.

Alex Schmitt, a college freshman at Michigan Tech University, spoke about his experiences with bullying during high school.

"My senior year of high school I was captain of the varsity hockey team. We were huge rivals with the other team in our town and would trash talk each other on the ice. It carried over to commenting on Facebook photos from hockey games, but it was harmless and went both ways."

"One night when my mom and sister were home, a group of boys came and T.P'ed our house. We never found out exactly who it was, but I had a pretty good idea."

"Another time when I was leaving for school, I walked out to my truck and saw that someone had thrown ice cream on the back window."

"I also got my truck keyed while it was parked in the school parking lot. I never found out exactly who did that either, though."

Although Alex did not experience any harm to himself, the actions against him were physical and more direct than would be seen among girls.

A national survey of children's exposure to violence found that, in 2008, boys were more likely to be victims of physical assault than girls. 50.2 percent of boys reported being physically assaulted within the previous year, compared with 42.1 percent of girls.

— *Samantha Schmitt*

CHAPTER 9

Girls' bullying can be almost secret

DAVID P. FARRINGTON, PROFESSOR of psychological criminology at Cambridge University, and other researchers agree that
females bully each other verbally and psychologically rather than
physically. This may have always been true, but the Internet and
the use of it by children of younger ages seems to have increased
the aggressiveness of attacks.

It is not always as easy to recognize bullying when it occurs
among girls.

"Cyberbullying," a 2007 report by Amanda Lenhart for the Pew
Internet and American Life Project, reported that girls are more
likely than boys to gossip online, making them more subject to
being the topic of online rumors.

In "Teenage Girls' Perceptions of the Functions of Relationally
Aggressive Behaviors," Bridget Reynolds and Rena Repetti said
that girls are more likely to be relationally aggressive. Relational
aggression is a subtle and indirect tactic used to attack relationships among friends and undermine self-esteem. It can include
rumors, denying friendships, ignoring or social exclusion.

In "Bullying: What are the Differences between Boys and Girls?"
Dr. Tanya Beran, professor of school psychology at the University
of Calgary, wrote that the secretive nature of this bullying may
mean the attacker does not get caught. The attacks are then likely
to become longer and can become more severe.

This kind of bullying is hard for adults to detect because its
indirect nature allows the bully to avoid face-to-face confrontation. Since it is usually hidden from adults, there is no physical
behavior to see.

Bullying among girls often happens within friendship groups, making it extremely difficult to differentiate it from a typical teenage conflict.

Kirstie Kipfmiller, a Michigan State senior, experienced bullying from friends in both elementary and high school.

"I was bullied in fifth grade for having buck-teeth. I hated it. It would make me so upset. I just didn't understand it, and it wasn't something that I could change at the time. Now, I have a great smile."

"More recently, in high school, particularly junior year, my class size was 36 kids. Some of my best friends and a majority of that class and upperclassmen turned on me. I've always been the girl that's 'one of the guys.' Well, this came with repercussions."

"Since I hung out with guys all of the time, I think girls got jealous, maybe? Certain people would make up rumors about me getting with all of these guys, calling me a slut, making up rumors about how I messed around with so many guys at one time. This lasted forever. I would cry in school."

"My so-called 'best friends' would even ignore me or just do hurtful things. I got sick of it. I decided I was better than that and ended up switching schools my senior year. It was the best decision ever. No one thought I would actually do that. I remember sitting there, crying in math class, and people would be like, 'Why don't you just go to John Glenn (another high school)?' I would look at them and say, 'Yeah, I will.' And I did it. Stupid kids."

"To this day, I still hang out with mostly guys. Being friends with girls is too hard. There's too much drama so I just stay away most of the time. I still get called a slut behind my back, but I grew up and realized that that stuff doesn't matter. I'm better than that, and I know who I am."

— *Samantha Schmitt*

CHAPTER 10

Aggressors need help, just like their targets

MOST DISCUSSIONS ABOUT BULLYING revolve around the targets of the bullying. However, there is another victim in this situation: the bully.

While the target can often get help, people who bully need help, too.

Bullies are often portrayed as dim-witted, large and overly aggressive, such as the cartoon characters Helga from Hey Arnold! and Roger from Doug. On the contrary, bullies can be intelligent, popular and highly charismatic. According to Education.com, a privately funded site, aggressors might also have traits of anger, aggression, hyperactivity and violence.

Just as victims might grow up to have issues later in life, bullies can also grow up to have unresolved problems. According to the anti-bullying organization Utterly Global, children who were bullies in grades six to nine are 60 percent more likely to have a criminal conviction by the age of 24. The organization reports that a bully is five times more likely than a victim to have a serious criminal record in adulthood. Even bullies who avoid the judicial system and grow up to work can cause problems at work. According to the National Institute for Occupational Safety and Health, workplace bullying causes $3 billion in lost productivity and a staggering $19 billion loss in employment every year.

Matt DeLisi, sociologist and head of the Iowa State University criminal justice program, wrote in an article for the ISU sociology department that, as bullies age, they are more likely to engage in antisocial behavior. According to DeLisi, adults who bullied as children are 10 times more likely to lie, six times more likely to fight and almost three times more likely to engage in harassment than adults who did not bully. "Bullies are 11 times more likely to have had conduct disorder than non-bullies. That giant fact shows you that bullies are antisocial anyway. When you get into personality disorders, you'll see that in antisocial personalities there is almost an eight times difference," wrote DeLisi.

The bullies themselves need help, just like their targets, to break the cycle. "Because bullies are so aggressive, they are viewed by peers to be so difficult to deal with, so they are rejected," writes DeLisi. Many bullies experience some type of abuse at home, and bullying others is simply a coping mechanism. Counseling can be provided as a way for bullies stop. As the global discussion about aggression grows, more attention is being paid to both the bullied and the bullies.

— *Devyne Lloyd*

PART 2
Cyberbullying

CHAPTER 11

Study shows teens' online world can have a mean streak

IN NOVEMBER 2011, A national report on teens' social media experiences gave a glimpse of what it feels like to be young and online.

"Teens, kindness and cruelty on social network sites," was written by the Pew Internet and American Life Project.

The study asked teens about their online experiences and how they respond when they see mean or unkind behavior. The targets of cyber aggression report that it affects their whole lives, making them anxious about going to school or leading to physical fights. Although some teens pile on while others turn to each other for help, most just don't get involved when they see online aggression.

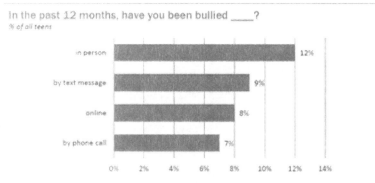

In the past 12 months, have you been bullied _____?
% of all teens

in person	12%
by text message	9%
online	8%
by phone call	7%

Source: The Pew Research Center's Internet & American Life Teen-Parent survey, April 26-July 14, 2011. n=799 for teens and parents, including oversample of minority families. Interviews were conducted in English and Spanish.

Source: The Pew Research Center

The study was based on telephone interviews with a representative sample of 799 U.S. teens aged 12 to 17 years old and their parents.

While most teens report positive online experiences, according to Pew, "some are caught in an online feedback loop of meanness and negative experiences."

Twenty percent flatly responded that their peers are mostly unkind, and an additional 11% responded "it depends."

Girls aged 12-13 active on social media were considerably more likely than other teens to say that people seemed to be mostly unkind. Thirty-three percent of them reported this to be their experience.

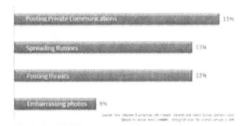

Some methods of cyberbullying are more
popular than others.

More than a quarter of all girls at this age said that they felt anxious about going to school the day after a bad online experience. Teens in other group reported anxieties, too.

While bullying continues to happen mostly in person, Pew reported that a substantial number of teens said they are bullied with technology. The study showed that 9 percent of teens aged 12-17 said they had been bullied by text, another 8 percent reported bullying by email, a social network site or instant messaging, and 7 percent said they have been bullied by phone.

A large majority of teens said they see digital bullying, even though they may not be its target. Eighty-eight percent told Pew they have seen peers being mean or cruel to others online. Twelve percent said this happens frequently. The report said teens who were not aware of much online cruelty are the ones who do not use social media very much.

About 55 percent of all teens said that the most frequent response of their peers to mean behavior online is to ignore it. Almost equal numbers — about 20 percent in each camp — said the responses they see to cruel behavior are to either tell someone to stop being mean or to join in the harassment.

The Pew report said teens might ignore mean behavior because it can be difficult to know what the aggression is all about and that some teens might ignore meanness to discourage it. It might also be that teens are intervening in private ways, such as direct messages.

— *Joe Grimm*

CHAPTER 12

Underage kids join Facebook, sometimes with parental help

KATIE SPRINGER HAD JUST joined the social networking website Facebook. She was 11 years old, two years younger than the site's minimum age requirement.

"Most of my friends were already on," she said, "so it wasn't a big deal."

Katie's mother, Karen, agreed to allow her to sign up for an account as long as Karen knew the password and could regularly check her activity.

It wasn't more than a few months before Katie started receiving taunts on Facebook from girls her age and in her neighborhood. One night, her classmates were so cruel that Karen was forced into action.

"The girls just wouldn't leave her alone," she said. "So I went and screamed at the parents of the one girl about what they were doing. Her defense was that kids will be kids."

Katie isn't alone. According to a poll conducted in January 2012 by Reuters News, 15 percent of American parents report that their child has been the victim of cyberbullying.

The impact of cyberbullying is felt by its victims. An MTV 2009 study of digital abuse indicated that eight percent of cyberbullying victims have had thoughts of suicide, compared to the three percent that have not been cyberbullied.

But Facebook is attempting to change that.

In March 2011, during the president's White House Conference on Bullying Prevention, Facebook rolled out new measures to help students who are being targeted by bullies on its site.

Now, if someone is being harassed or bullied, they may contact a third party who can help with the situation.

Joe Sullivan, Facebook's chief security officer, explained the changes at the White House Conference.

"We also want to encourage individuals to stand up and to share that bad content with someone in their life that they think can help them," said Sullivan. "The idea is that when you go to report something on Facebook, you can tell a trusted friend who can act as an intermediary or advise you on the situation."

The individual being bullied chooses the friend to whom they will report the abuse.

Facebook offers three strategies for dealing with online harassment:

- Don't respond. Typically, bullies want to get a response — don't give them one.
- Don't keep it a secret. Use Facebook's Trusted Friend tool to send a copy of the abusive content to someone you trust who can help you deal with the bullying. This will also generate a report to Facebook.
- Do document and save. If the attacks persist, you may need to report the activity to a parent or educator and they will want to see the messages.

To some, there is still more to be done to combat cyberbullying on Facebook.

Members of the Federation of Parents and Citizens associations in New South Wales, New Zealand, would like to see classes for youth on how to properly use Facebook and other websites, and how to deal with online bullying.

In a July 2011 interview, Thomas Tudehope, a representative of the organization, said, "The lack of adequate social media education is glaringly obvious as each week brings a new social media scandal reverberating through the Web and mainstream media."

— *Dustin Petty*

CHAPTER 13

Internet bullying has become a social norm

AT A RALLY PLANNED to coincide with an advance screening of the movie Bully, one college volunteer spoke about fake Facebook accounts that students at her high school had used to bully others. Another college volunteer, who went to a different high school said, "Ah, high school memories."

Online aggression appears to be widespread and it can be anonymous.

Trishie Schweinfurth, class of 2014 at Deerfield High School in Illinois, checks her Facebook, cell phone, Tumblr and email at least three times a day to talk to friends and to "stay in the loop."

"My friends and I made a fake AIM screen name when we were in seventh grade to mess with another girl in our grade," Schweinfurth said.

She doesn't, however, consider this bullying.

"I have been bullied and I have bullied," she said.

"A lot of things are considered to be bullying today which I feel like I fall under the category of 'semi-bullying.' I know my friends and I have judged people for what they are wearing," she said.

Schweinfurth says she herself has received comments like "Why would you wear that?" and "What were you thinking?"

At Deerfield High School, the "popular girls" call themselves "DA GURLZ" and even made a Facebook group with this name.

"They said anything and everything because they thought that they were the only ones that were able to see these horrific things they would say about people," said Schweinfurth.

But nothing on the Internet is ever private.

"After a while, someone left their Facebook on at someone else's house and the password got exposed to the whole school and everyone went on to see if DA GURLZ had said anything about them," said Schweinfurth.

The Internet may have become a popular way for high school students to bully each other, but it does not always stay anonymous and it is not without its consequences.

— *Hayley Beitman*

CHAPTER 14

Researcher draws line between bullying and online drama

WHILE ADULTS REFER TO arguments and gossip on social media as bullying, teens simply call it drama.

Danah Boyd, a senior researcher with Microsoft who works to prove the Internet is actually a safe place for teens, and Alice Marwick, a postdoctoral researcher, spent six years doing interviews for the paper "The Drama! Teen Conflict, Gossip, and Bullying in Networked Publics," published in September of 2011.

According to their paper: "When American teens talk about their day-to-day lives, drama invariably comes up. Drama is the language that teens—most notably girls—use to describe a host of activities and practices ranging from gossip, flirting, arguing, and joking to more serious issues of jealousy, ostracization, and name-calling."

Danah Boyd at the Writers on Writing about Technology Conference at Yale in 2009. Photo by Sage Ross, published under Creative Commons license.

Boyd said there is a "gendered difference to meanness and cruelty."

"Girls are more likely to engage in 'relational aggression' — gossip-mongering, rumor-spreading, etc. — while boys are more likely to engage in physical aggression or to engage in punking or pranking that can be hurtful," she said.

According to the paper, drama is different from bullying.

In the paper, Boyd and Marwick define drama's five key components: it is social and interpersonal, it involves relational conflict, it is reciprocal, it is gendered and is often performed for, in, and magnified by networked publics.

Drama is different from bullying because drama is social and interpersonal. Teens can avoid drama by not engaging, but they cannot avoid bullying. Drama can also go on within the same friend group, which is different than bullying, Boyd wrote.

According to Boyd, the Internet has not increased bullying, but social media helps increase drama.

"Actually, the data has consistently shown that bullying has not increased with the rise of the Internet. In fact, there's fantastic data that shows that young people report that face-to-face bullying happens more frequently, does more psychological damage, and is more difficult to deal with than what happens online," she said. "What happens through technology is more visible to more people, including adults. Bullying does not encompass all forms of meanness and cruelty. Bullying specifically refers to social, physical or psychological aggression that is repeated over time between people of different social standing or physical stature. Most of what happens online is reciprocated meanness and cruelty that escalates. That's an entirely different set of dynamics."

— *Alethia Kasben*

CHAPTER 15

Griefers stalk players in video games

ANDREW, 16 AND IN 10th grade, plays Minecraft at least an hour every day, usually after school. He spends his time building virtual castles and complex machinery in a game that combines the creative power of building blocks and the role-playing element of a video game. Most of the time, he and his friends play on servers where they are protected from griefers.

A griefer is a bully in the world of online games. Griefers don't play by the rules and attempt to cause as much distress and discomfort for other players as possible.

In Minecraft, griefers go after the creations of other players.

"I've seen seven hours of work get completely destroyed," Andrew said.

Though many servers have griefer protections in place, those protections sometimes get in the way of regular players, Andrew said. Sometimes, playing against a griefer can be fun, since it becomes a competition and the game suddenly has a villain. Other times, griefers trick their way into becoming administrators of a server and destroying everything the players have built, which could waste weeks of work.

Andrew admits to having griefed himself. It can be fun, he said.

Minecraft players can become quite attached to their creations, especially as it takes many

One of Andrew's constructions

days, sometimes months, to create particularly complex or large structures.

These creations are important to the players, even though they are virtual, Andrew said. Though it's not quite on the same level as his real-life possessions, he and other Minecraft players are upset when their work is destroyed.

According to Mike Ambinder, an experimental psychologist at Valve Software in Bellevue, Wash., many people get pleasure from griefing others, and it often becomes a competition among them to see who can cause the most chaos.

Griefing can be very similar to bullying, as Andrew and Ambinder attest.

"The mob mentality is a phenomenon that has been extensively studied and definitely seems to be at play here," Ambinder said.

The more players are engaged in destructive behavior, the more likely others are to join.

As with other forms of bullying, players sometimes get singled out and picked on.

"When people don't know each other personally, that will never happen," Andrew said, referring to the server he and his friends run, but he admits that things are probably different on large, public servers.

There have been griefing concerns in a bigger game. Recently, World of Warcraft and the company that produces it, Blizzard, have come under fire for being lax on cyberbullying.

World of Warcraft forums are full of players complaining that they have been repeat-

Wooden structures are particularly vulnerable to fire, as griefers know.

edly harassed, to the point where they've quit the game. Despite cyberbullying being against Blizzard's terms of use, it is tough to report and punish the bullies. The game's enormous player base

-- more than 10 million subscribers in 2011 -- makes strict control difficult.

Cyberbullying is recognized as a legitimate threat on social networks, but video games are often battlegrounds for the same kind of behavior. One World of Warcraft player complained on the forums that a group of players was harassing people by impersonating players and bothering others, bringing blame on their targets. This is similar to Facebook cyberbullying when high school students create fake profiles of fellow students. They then post humiliating information about them, or harass others under their assumed name.

Controlling and preventing griefing is difficult. In World of Warcraft, moderators attempt to ban bullies, but they can't get them all, because there are so many players. Minecraft servers can be protected against griefers, but safeguards interfere with legitimate play.

Not all Minecraft servers are protected from griefers.

"I think it should be individually up to every server or person," Andrew said.

Even if the server has anti-griefer measures, truly determined players will download modifications to the game that allow them to bypass protections.

Minecraft Animals

"Research -- our own and that done by psychologists 'in the wild' -- seems to confirm that incentivizing positive behavior is stronger and leads to longer-lasting effects than punishing negative behavior," Ambinder said.

At the end of the day, griefing hurts video games and gamers, Ambinder said, and Valve is working to discourage it.

As for Andrew, he will continue building and protecting his creations, hidden away on a private server.

— Dmitri Barvinok

CHAPTER 16

A second look at "Bully:" The video game

"BULLY," A VIDEO GAME produced by Rockstar Games, was greeted by panic and protest by many organizations. Jack Thompson, an infamous anti-gaming activist, went as far as to compare the game to Columbine. "Bully" made both the Yahoo! list of Top 10 controversial games, and PlayStation Magazine's Top 10 Games of 2006. Lawsuits were filed in an attempt to prevent the sale of the game.

Two years after the original game went on sale, an extended version titled "Bully: Scholarship Edition" was released, and this time around, it was greeted with praise, not subpoenas.

The game follows the story of Jimmy Hopkins, a boy from a family with a remarried mother and an absent father, who ends up at Bullworth Academy, a no-nonsense private school teeming with bullies in every corner.

Daniel Moon picked the game up after it went on sale. He doesn't believe it warranted the controversial press that accompanied its release. He said that a player is not required to be a bully in the game, but can make that choice.

"(However), the content in the game does require violence," he added, "because, well, it's a Rockstar game."

Rockstar is best known for the "Grand Theft Auto" games.

As Jimmy, you can make friends, though you'll most likely make enemies, go to class — or if you don't, try to avoid the consequences — and rise through the social ranks of the school, occasionally bullying, and occasionally helping others.

"Bully" contains school violence and suggestive themes, but it is a far cry from Columbine, or any extraordinary school violence. Jimmy does have a slingshot, but the only gun in the game shoots potatoes. Nothing is lethal, though it could get gross when stink bombs and itching powder are involved.

Set in the time before cell phones and cyberbullying, "Bully" brings the player back to the time when the locker room was the most dangerous place to be, and the library was a haven. Though the methods are primitive, it paints bullying as a social tool, something bullies use to gain power in their social circles.

In the game, Jimmy is always at odds with Gary, a boy that pretends to be his friend, but who begins to sabotage him, trying to get him expelled.

"There can be a true friendship and then in order to 'keep' that friendship, you have one person begin to control the other," said anti-bullying activist Kevin Epling. "This then becomes a normal thing as one person exerts their authority over the other person."

Relying on school stereotypes and cliques, "Bully" nonetheless treats bullying as a multidimensional issue, focusing on both targets and bullies.

According to Moon, the game doesn't go far enough to show a realistic picture of bullying.

"It lacks the emotional aspect of feeling like everything is going wrong," he said, "The character, despite getting into bullied positions, has that angst and arrogance to drive him. Most bullied victims don't."

— *Dmitri Barvinok*

CHAPTER 17

America is not alone in dealing with the issue

AMERICANS HAVE BEEN PAYING more attention to bullying over the past 10 years.

Laws, conferences, research and conversation have proliferated. But the issue is not just an American one. Much of the world is concerned about bullying. Take the example of a bullying incident that occurred in Australia in March, 2011:

"We had an incident here last March when a school bully got beaten up by his victim, and the video of the incident went viral," said Scott Parlett, a student at the University of New South Wales. "All of the television networks worked to put their own spin on the event, including interviews with parents and the kid who recorded the fight."

Scan the code with a QR-reader to see the viral video, or go to http://www.you-tube.com/watch?v=isfn4OxCPQs&.

The 42-second YouTube clip of the fight had more than 7 million views in April 2012. Although there are some who believe that Casey Heynes, the initial victim of the bully, was wrong to retaliate, the consensus seems to be that he was a hero for standing up to the bully.

"Casey has now transferred schools and is classified by others as a true hero thanks to publicity and being able to fight against bullying," said Kate Giulano, a student at the University of Newcastle.

"Justin Bieber was touring Australia when this happened and he flew Casey and his family to his Melbourne show and got Casey up on stage during the performance to explain to the audience how much of a hero Casey was for standing up to bullying."

Parlett said that technology has changed the way the two students, watched from around the world, will move on from this incident.

"Unfortunately for Ritchard and Casey, the two boys involved in the incident, we are in this new technological world so that their 30-second fight went viral and will continue to reappear throughout their lives," Parlett said. "The initial bully in this case is now sometimes seen as the victim because of the video going viral as everyone tries to have their two cents worth in commenting."

Parlett has seen how technology is changing bullying. "I see bullying like a never-ending spring. The bullying continues as the victims fight back and then they become bullies, and the initial bullies become victims, especially in the new technological world with the Internet," Parlett said.

"Fortunately, when I was bullied there was not camera phones, the town I grew up in was so small that everyone knows everything. This is one of the reasons why I left my hometown to further my education. I hated that everyone knew everything about you," Parlett said. "Today, it doesn't matter. You can't escape what happens because it's posted for all to see online."

Interest in bullying has increased markedly worldwide. News reference graphs on Google display how interest in the subject has increased dramatically in the past few years.

While bullying seems to be a frequent news item in America, the United States ranks 10th in the world for Web searches on the subject. This shows that bullying is a worldwide issue. The millions of view on the video from an Australian schoolyard shows that the content does not stay within national boundaries.

According to research published in Psychology Science Quarterly in 2009, America trails several countries in bullying incidents. Europeans struggle with the issue as much, if not more than Americans.

Research conducted in Germany showed that more than 18 percent of students between the ages of six and 19 are affected by bullying, with an additional five percent being impacted by cyber-bullying. Recent news reports coming out of Germany describe the vicious nature of some attacks in schools.

Tolgahan Dilgin, a Ph.D. student in political science at Michigan State University who is originally from Turkey, recalled bullying he saw in Germany as a youth.

"As a teenager, you know, they aren't always the happiest of people, so I was questioning life and the world and everything. I was asking myself, 'Has humanity died? What's going on?' " Dilgin said. "The summer when I was 14 or 15, I went to Germany for a youth camp, and then I found the answer to my question. Yes, humanity has died."

Dilgin said that the bullying he encountered in Germany was beyond his imagination.

"I hadn't seen anything like that, and I just felt ashamed witnessing it. There was one kid specifically picked on, they only called him a word that basically meant ugly," Dilgin said. "That wasn't even the worst part. When that kid was outside of the camp they would pee and masturbate on his bed."

Dilgin said that he usually tried to be as inclusive as possible as a child growing up, but while he was in Germany, he was unable to step in and prevent bullying. "I realized you can only stop these things when you are in your own country and your own culture. You can't step in when you are in a foreign culture and you're an outsider," Dilgin said. "We were too busy protecting ourselves because we were getting made fun of also. In comparison to that kid though, ours was just like, OK, this is their culture and they're rough."

Dr. Leonhard Thun-Hohenstein, head of child psychiatry at the Christian Doppler Hospital on the border between Germany and Austria, was cited in an article on Deutsche-Presse Agentur as saying that children need much more thorough care as opposed to traditional counseling when they are victims of bullying.

"In some cases, we are having to admit pupils for inhouse psychiatric care, not just outpatient counseling. We handle up to a dozen young people a year on an inpatient basis, which is extraordinary in itself," Thun-Hohenstein said in the article.

"These are children and young adults suffering from acute depression and in some cases suicidal tendencies," he said. "They just can't face going back to school."

— *Tommy Franz*

PART 3
Hazing

CHAPTER 18

The crime of hazing

CLOSE BEHIND THE EFFORT to outlaw bullying is the effort to criminalize hazing, and not just in the United States. The Philippines has a national anti-hazing law. In the United States, hazing is regulated at the state and local levels.

Hazing laws vary by state, and a collective definition does not yet exist. Jacinda Boucher, author of "Hazing and Higher Education," defines hazing as encompassing "an extensive range of behaviors and activities, ranging from seemingly innocuous activities such as blindfolding and scavenger hunts, to more dangerous and extreme physical punishments, including sleep deprivation and excessive exercise."

Hank Nuwer, hazing author and public speaker, defines bullying as mean or dangerous behavior meant to exclude someone from a group. His contrasting definition of hazing is bringing someone into a group, even if the initiation rites are silly or demeaning. The problem, according to Nuwer,

Glenn R. Stutzky, clinical instructor, Michigan State University School of Social Work.

is that hazing can also be bullying, for example when a football team does not want someone to join.

Glen R. Stutzky, clinical instructor in the School of Social Work at Michigan State University, defines hazing as group bullying. Everyone's definition is a little different.

Attending college leaves many students looking for a sense of belonging. This is a time when senior members of organizations have the opportunity to initiate new members into their group the same way they were initiated. According to Stutzky, this is wrong for the people in charge and for the people who submit to hazing to become members.

According to one of the largest national hazing surveys, coordinated by Dr. Nadine C. Hoover of Alfred University, hazing is widespread. The study included more than 60,000 student athletes from 2,400 colleges and universities. It found "over 325,000 athletes at more than 1,000 National Collegiate Athletic Association schools participated in intercollegiate sports during 1998-99. Of these athletes, more than a quarter of a million (250,000+) experienced some form of hazing to join a college athletic team."

Hoover said, "One in five was subjected to unacceptable and potentially illegal hazing. They were kidnapped, beaten or tied up and abandoned. They were also forced to commit crimes, destroying property, making prank phone calls or harassing others."

A large number of universities have recently developed hazing laws due to public pressures. According to Nuwer, 44 states have laws forbidding hazing, with Alaska, Hawaii, Montana, New Mexico, South Dakota, and Wyoming being exceptions. Opponents of hazing laws have argued that the term is too general, that hazing is perpetual or too hard to prove without physical proof.

According to the Cincinnati law firm of Manley Burke, while hazing punishments vary, most states consider it to be a misdemeanor punishable by fines of up to $5,000. The problem states have is that incidents are rarely reported. Nuwer said that working toward a federal law is critical to solving the problem and encouraging sufficient reporting.

Massachusetts is working toward mandatory reporting of hazing. Florida and New Hampshire have some of the most advanced hazing laws. Florida has three laws to manage hazing at universities and colleges, both public and private, while New Hampshire classifies hazing as a misdemeanor.

According to The Greek Shop website, in Illinois, Idaho, Missouri, Texas, Virginia and Wisconsin, fatal hazing or hazing inflicting bodily harm is considered a felony. Some states, including Alabama, Ohio, Oklahoma and Rhode Island, recognize the mental and physical harms of hazing. Stutzky said most hazing injuries are not physical, but mental and emotional. Delaware, Pennsylvania and Tennessee require colleges to have written hazing policies. Florida and Kentucky require written hazing laws with punishments.

The Alfred University study said hazing is most likely to occur on campuses in eastern or southern states. Eastern and western states have the most alcohol-related hazing while southern and western states have the most dangerous hazing. Women are most likely to be involved with alcohol-related hazing. Male athletes who play soccer, lacrosse, swim or dive are most at risk for hazing in general, while football players are most likely to be dangerously or illegally hazed. The study found athletes and coaches agree on a few ways to prevent hazing. They include introducing clear anti-hazing messages, expect responsibility from athletes, and offer team bonding supervised by a coach.

It seems a combination of strictness from Greek national offices and high schools is the next step in hazing regulation. These areas would likely focus on early-stage hazing prevention rather than on minimizing individual liability. Nuwer said education is the most important way to combat hazing because if bystanders step in, others will too.

— *Hayley Beitman*

CHAPTER 19

Band hazing is facing tighter scrutiny and new laws

BANDS ARE WELL KNOWN for initiations. New members come in under the old members, do as they're told and at some point they hopefully become full members with full benefits.

The continued success of an organization depends on the knowledge, dedication and traditions of its members. However, numerous reports find that collegiate and even high school band initiations involve physical and mental abuse.

That is hazing.

Robert Champion, a former drum major in the marching band at Florida Agricultural and Mechanical University, died from shock due to severe blood loss during a hazing ritual for the band fraternity Kappa Kappa Psi, Inc., in November 2011. Several FAMU band members were suspended and charged after a girl's thigh bone was broken in half while they were beating her with instruments during another hazing ritual around November 2011. In 2006, the University of Wisconsin band was put on probation after a hazing incident involving alcohol abuse and sexual misconduct during a band trip. That prompted the assistant band director to resign. In 2008, the band was suspended for hazing incidents mirroring what happened in 2006.

In some cases, hazing continues to occur even after someone is hurt. Band hazing can also carry over from high school to college.

After Champion's death, his former high school in Georgia and 21 other Georgia high schools were investigated.

Michael Cage, a former band member at Martin Luther King Jr. High School in Detroit, experienced hazing while trying to get into the band in 2004.

"We got crab names, had to wear the crab uniforms, we got picked on, took wood on occasion but it never got out of hand," he said. "It was fun to me and I can honestly say that I didn't mind it at all."

Cage's experience was cut short, however, after the Detroit Public Schools moved to end hazing in organizations.

The 2010-2011 Detroit Public Schools Code of Conduct classifies bullying, intimidation, harassment and hazing as offenses punishable by short-term suspension, long-term suspension for high school students and administrative transfer. It all depends on the severity of the incident.

Does it still happen?

A student in a Detroit public high school, who asked to remain anonymous, said he was hazed while trying to join the band in the fall of 2011.

"There's things you've got to do while you're a crab," he said. "It's called brotherhood. I wasn't really hazed, though, because I knew what I had to do to get to the level I'm at now."

Both students say that hazing isn't necessarily a bad thing and if the crabs do what they are told and learn what they are supposed to learn in a timely fashion, the process will go by quickly and will not get out of hand.

Michigan State University alumnus Bryan Cotton – a member of the college fraternity Alpha Phi Alpha Fraternity, Inc. – said he sees a connection between band hazing, such as Champion's case, and the hazing that takes place in college fraternities and sororities.

"I feel as though there is an obvious relation between the two," he said. "Fraternities and sororities have always been documented in hazing cases and faced constant ridicule for their practices."

Cotton said the constant focus on hazing in fraternities and sororities allowed bands to carry out hazing rituals without much scrutiny, picking up many rituals from them. That is starting to change.

"Now everyone has to watch their back," said Cotton.

According to Elizabeth J. Allan and Marry Madden from the University of Maine College of Education and Human Development, 73 percent of college students who are in a sorority or fraternity experience at least one hazing behavior, while 56 percent of members of a performing arts organization, such as bands, experience hazing at least once.

Bowie State history graduate Joseph Harris, also a member of Alpha Phi Alpha Fraternity, Inc., says that the link goes deeper. "To truly understand hazing in relation to Greek life (college fraternities and sororities) and bands, you have to examine the issue at its roots," said Harris. "Greeks started it, but then those who were Greek and also members of the band passed it on within those confines."

Consensual hazing, however, is still illegal.

"In states that have laws against hazing, consent of the victim is not a defense," according to PreventHazing.ku.edu at the University of Kansas. Intimidation, threats, peer pressure and the desire for inclusion can all play a part in the victim's "consent," but the argument won't hold a note with a judge.

Michigan State junior band member Auston McMurray, who said he has never been hazed himself, feels that hazing is a tradition that will be difficult to change.

"It's so ingrained in band culture that it will take a collective mindset and effort from everyone to stop it," he said. "The effort has to start now, though. The sooner the better."

— *Devyne Lloyd and Allen Martin*

CHAPTER 20

Hazing liaison brings the issues out into the open

IN 2008 THE UNIVERSITY of Wisconsin-Madison marching band was suspended for hazing. The allegations involved alcohol and inappropriate sexual behavior. It was the first time the band missed a home game in Band Director Mike Leckrone's 42-year tenure.

Donna Freitag, the former women's basketball coach, was brought in as a band liaison to help combat hazing in the band.

One of the first things Freitag said she did was conduct leadership training with rank leaders and band members of the band.

"An upperclassmen is assigned an incoming freshman to mentor and help them transition into college and into the band," she said. "They are another outlet for them to communicate with if they feel there is a problem with the band."

During the training, a group also tightened the code of conduct, which was lax in areas of hazing and drinking on the road, she said. "We want to teach them to be better leaders and solidify team building." Freitag said that

Donna Freitag became band liason at the University of Wisconsin-Madison following hazing incidents.

hazing, even in its simplest forms, can lead to dangerous traditions, and that initiations should not be meant to embarrass new members.

In early 2012, Freitag talked about her work with the band and the progress it has made in the past three years:

How did you receive the position as band liaison?

"After I retired from coaching in April of 2008, I had done a lot of networking on campus. I had known a lot of people on campus. I knew I wanted to stay on. I was in my high school marching band, so I had a band background as well. Through word of mouth, I was contacted."

Did you ever deal with hazing as a basketball coach?

"Now that I look back, I think there were some hazing incidents that seemed pretty minimal. There was a freshman skip in front of the team as entertainment for the team. At a lower level, it is still hazing."

Do you think there are differences in hazing based on gender or institution?

"I think there is potentially a difference between men and women in regards to hazing. Men can be a little more physical. Women can do hazing in emotional type ways: ignoring them, treating them like crap, cleaning the sorority all night long and not getting any sleep. Men use more beating and excessive drinking; more violent activities."

What have you been doing to try and end hazing?

"One of the things I did immediately, I met with all the freshmen and newcomers, there were about 80. I met with them individually, asked how their experience was going to establish trust, so they knew they had someone to go to that first year. Then I started meeting with all the rank and section leaders. I met with 190 band students from October until the end of the semester. I was busy. But I felt that it was important I connect with them and find out what the culture was all about. I wanted to find out what they were all about and what was happening. From those meetings

I learned who those leaders were. I ran into some who felt like what was happening was a part of the band, they were fun and didn't feel like there was anything wrong with it. The ones I was looking for were the change agents of the band."

Is it working?

"I think it is working very well. It would be foolish to think we are never going to have any problems. We have gotten to the point now where if there is an incident it is an isolated incident. We have made some huge strides. We talk about communication between ranks, the chain of command in regards to who band students can go to if there are problems. What happened three years ago is that everyone was so quiet. This is life, but it's how we deal with it from now on. "

Band hazing has been called a part of the culture, is that true?

"Wisconsin and Midwest students know quite a bit about the band. They come here and sometimes you do things because you think you have to and you just want to be a part of it so bad. It could happen between ranks, each section of the band, each field has their own system of behavior. They (alumni) talk a lot about it as a tradition, alumni pressure that creates this atmosphere that they want it to continue."

Will it ever end?

"I don't think it will completely ever stop. There will always be some sort of initiation. Whenever you bring in new members there is always a change. I hope the extent will go down and welcoming new members become more positive. Initiations can always happen, but I think the activity needs to change. Is it to truly get to know them or is it to belittle and embarrass them in front of the upperclassman?"

What do you think can be done at the high school level to end hazing?

"Band directors need to be aware of it and not hide from it. Maybe they also have a new-member orientation and hazing workshop. Give examples of what could happen. I think again, sticking your head in the sand isn't going to change anything. Whether it is severe in their band or not, I think we need to communicate it and be proactive and nab it right away."

— *Alethia Kasben*

CHAPTER 21

At many levels, sports teams are trying to cut the hazing

HAZING RITUALS, LONG A part of some college and high school sports teams, are getting more scrutiny.

The National Collegiate Athletic Association (NCAA), which governs college sports, now monitors hazing.

In 2007, the NCAA published, "Building New Traditions: Hazing Prevention in College Athletics." The report outlines roles for everyone involved with collegiate athletics, ranging from school administrators to coaches and players. Recognizing behaviors of the past, the NCAA recommended a departmental approach to hazing prevention.

"The effort to create a change in attitudes and behavior will be worth the effort if it prevents one student-athlete from a humiliating or degrading experience, physical injury or psychological harm, as a result of a hazing incident," according to the report.

The need to prevent bullying is being discussed at the high school level, as well.

In Pennsylvania, Upper Dublin High School, 9th grade basketball coach Alex Schugsta says hazing occurs in other schools, but it is not something he wants around his team. "To me, it seems to contradict the entire team concept behind sports. I fail to see how it builds team chemistry by alienating one or a few players on a team," says Schugsta, a former high school basketball player. "An acceptable sports bonding practice would be a pizza and movie activity, or if time and money permits, perhaps a paint-balling day. Activities like this build the team concept and sense of togetherness," says Schugsta.

Hazing as a rite of sports passage is not just a problem in the United States. Luke Lichtenstein, a former high school basketball player in Sydney, Australia, says hazing is present in Australian high school sports the same way it is in the United States. "There definitely were cliques within teams, but it never got to the point where a teammate would ever feel pressured to do something just to fit in," Lichtenstein said. "I was taught that having multiple members from a team pressuring a fellow teammate to do something they don't want to do goes against the whole concept of being a team."

Team building is the central theme, according Dirk Roberts, former football graduate assistant at Salem High School in Michigan. When talking about hazing on his football team, he was adamant that, "We didn't allow that stuff to happen. We didn't want to see any of it." The topic of hazing in sports is a taboo topic, but Roberts said, "I can understand where it fits in, but you have to draw the line somewhere."

NCAA defines hazing as, "Any act committed against someone joining or becoming a member or maintaining membership in any organization that is humiliating, intimidating or demeaning, or endangers the health and safety of the person."

While the NCAA provides a definition for hazing, the practice itself is so broad that it is difficult to establish a universal definition for hazing in sports. Someone must carry the water cooler, but is it hazing if only the new members of the team have to do it? Someone needs to pick up the basketballs after practice, but is it hazing if only the rookies do it? Those are the questions coaches and team leaders face at every practice. While some coaches may see that "there's the tradition behind it," other coaches take a zero-tolerance attitude.

NCAA's approach is like Schugsta's. The boundary between hazing and team-building is a fine line. "Hazing is a power trip . . . team building is a shared, positive experience," said the NCAA.

The NCAA report on "Building New Traditions: Hazing Prevention in College Athletics" can be found online.

— *Seth Beifel*

CHAPTER 22

Bully coaches in sports affect young athletes

FOR ANY SPORTS ENTHUSIAST, it's an image ingrained in their memories. As Steve Reid, a Purdue Boilmakers men's basketball player, stepped to the line to shoot two free throws in a game against Indiana in 1985, a red blur suddenly darted toward him. As the blur got closer to Reid, he realized it was a sideline chair that Indiana Head Coach Bob Knight had thrown toward him.

It was at this moment that Knight, known for his aggressive and sometimes over the top tactics, became the most infamous coaching bully in sports.

While Knight may be the most notorious bully figure in sports, he is not the only one.

"You would be surprised at the amount of bullying that goes on by coaches in youth sports," said Dr. Patrick Cohn, who specializes in youth sports psychology. "75 percent of kids drop out of sport by the time they are 15, and it is accredited to not having fun. If they are being bullied and not having fun the chance of dropping out is greater."

While Knight's chair throwing incident happened to collegiate athletes, similar incidents happening to young athletes can have severe psychological effects.

According to Cohn, bullied kids are deflated and lack comfort and security in sports. In some cases, he says that believe that they performed poorly and they are the reason for the coaches behavior.

"Coaches have a lot of power because unlike the mandatory taking of classes, athletics is a choice," said Carl Pickhardt, a Ph.D. psychologist and our bullying expert. "Children are there because they want to play and the coach sets the terms for how you play. You follow their rules."

How exactly do you know what makes a coach a bully?

According to the National Council for Accreditation of Coaching Education, a bully coach is someone who uses verbal or physical intimidation to motivate athletes.

"Coaches walk the line of being too enthusiastic and crossing over to pushing a child into something they aren't ready for or isn't age appropriate," NCACE Executive Director Christopher Hickey said.

While many parents struggle with dealing with coaches who may be bullying their child, Pickhardt says that there are three possible steps in dealing with the situation.

First, the parents have to sit down with the child and determine whether the treatment they are getting from the coach is personal, or if it is just a coach's harder operating style that is universal to the whole team.

After you they sit down with the child, Pickhardt says the next step is to determine that the bullying is not about anything wrong with the player, and it is something wrong with the coach. If it is determined that there is something wrong with the coach, the parent needs to get the permission of the child to talk to the coach.

The third and final step requires the parent to request to sit down and talk with the coach. It is better to set up a time and place to talk, rather than talking after an incident when your emotions are still running high.

Many parents are afraid to confront coaches because they see that as a sure way to eliminate any playing time their child might be getting. Hickey however, says that there is one important message that all parents need to be aware of.

"Parents need to realize that whenever something is wrong with their child, they need to step up and say something immediately," he said. "You might be talking about playing time today, but if your child is on a team where the adult is the bully, your child isn't going to be playing the sport for very long because it isn't going to be any fun."

—*Colby Berthume*

CHAPTER 23

Workplace bullying, long studied in Europe, gets noticed in U.S.

"IT'S LIKE EVERY DAY is Monday," said one executive assistant who works for an insurance firm in New York City.

"I just dread going to work and my work days seem endless."

She feels she is the target of a workplace bully. Work projects get delayed by her boss but the delay is publicly blamed on her. She will often come to work an hour or two early at his request only to find that he hasn't completed his part of the project or, worse, he isn't coming in at all. Conversely, he will impulsively demand that she stay late, and if she can't due to other commitments, he will complain about her lack of dedication. He has complained to human resources many times.

This executive assistant is one of an estimated 53.5 million Americans, or 35 percent of the U.S. workforce, who are bullied at work each year, according to the Workplace Bullying Institute, an organization created 15 years ago to study workplace bullying and advocate for its remedy.

According to the Society for Human Resource Management, workplace bullying is "persistent, offensive, abusive, intimidating or insulting behavior or unfair actions directed at another individual, causing the recipient to feel threatened, abused, humiliated or vulnerable."

"A long time ago, I worked for someone who sexually harassed me," said the assistant. "I would rather be sexually harassed than this. There are clear rules about that and laws against it. I am so stressed out, it is making me ill. I have been sicker this past year than I have ever been in my entire life."

The detrimental physical effects of bullying in the workplace are well documented. In a 2003 Workplace Bullying Institute study, for instance, 45 percent of those who are targets of workplace bullying experienced "stress-related health problems, debilitating anxiety, panic attacks, clinical depression (39 percent) and even post-traumatic stress disorder (30 percent of women; 21 percent of men)."

Furthermore, the stress of workplace bullying takes place not just once, but over time. A 2007 Zogby International poll found that "73 percent of bullied targets endure bullying for more than six months, 44 percent for at least one year." Zogby International, a market research and public opinion firm, has partnered with the Workplace Bullying Institute in its research.

"Workplace bullying is an organizational cultural problem," said Catherine Mattice, president of Civility Partners, LLC, in San Diego, Calif., a professional consulting and training firm that helps companies build a positive and civil workplace.

"Any time you have an organization where people do not get along," Mattice said, "It hurts them and then it hurts the teamwork and the ability to communicate and that hurts a company's bottom line."

In a recent survey by the Society for Human Resource Management, 51 percent of the companies surveyed reported incidents of bullying and 87 percent of the respondents (most of them HR professionals) believe that HR should handle bullying complaints.

Catherine Mattice, President Principal Consultant and Trainer at Civility Partners, LLC.

HR departments of large and small companies have been tasked to develop and implement strategies and policies to prevent all types of workplace abuse including race, sex and age discrimination, and sexual harassment. According to the Society for Human Resource Management report, however, 44 percent of companies do not currently have a "formal (written, documented) workplace bullying policy." Of the 40 percent that do have a policy, workplace bullying is included in another policy.

Employee policy handbooks have become so extensive that most companies will require new hires to review the policy handbook on their own and sign an affidavit indicating that they have read, reviewed and agreed to abide by the policies.

"Most of the onboarding functions are done online now," said Shari Funk, an HR generalist at Citigroup for 14 years. "I touch on the things that I think are really important to highlight to people like electronic communication processes, making sure that they are using email appropriately, and behavior in the office."

Not all HR professionals believe workplace bullying is a problem.

"When I speak to some HR professionals or at some HR meetings," said Mattice, "there are inevitably a few in the audience who don't just disagree with me, they really aggressively disagree with me."

"Workplace bullying is the new thing," said Mattice. "As businesses start using the term more frequently, the resistance will stop."

But workplace bullying has a long history. It's just been called other things like harassment, psychological terrorization, horizontal violence or simply conflict. In Europe and America, it is known as mobbing when two or more people join in bullying the target.

Psychologists and therapists in Europe during the 1980s were the first to take notice of and study the connection between bullying behaviors at work and the psychological damage they saw in their patients. Sweden and England in particular were in the vanguard of this research.

The first book devoted to the subject, "Bullying at Work: How to Confront and Overcome It" (1992), was written by British broadcaster and journalist Andrea Adams. Tim Field, who in 2001 would co-author the book "Bullycide: Death at Playtime," also in the United Kingdom, which brought media attention to childhood bullying and suicide, campaigned against bullying at work before he turned his attention to schools

After a breakdown he attributed to being bullied by a colleague, Field started his anti-bullying campaign with a workplace bullying website called the UK National Workplace Hotline which, he reported, has received more than one million visits since its inception until just 2005.

The work that these and other anti-workplace bullying advocates have done on this topic has led to strong legislation against workplace bullying and mobbing in Europe, again, particularly in Sweden and England.

In America, the Workplace Bullying Institute was created by Gary and Ruth Namie in the late 1990s as "the first and only organization that integrates all aspects of workplace bullying: self-help advice for individuals, personal coaching, research, public education, union assistance, training for professionals, employer consulting, and legislative advocacy."

Legislators are beginning to take notice of their efforts. On May 12, 2010, New York became the ninth state to pass a workplace bullying bill. The bill passed in the New York Senate, 45-16, but stalled in the house.

The Healthy Workplace Bill would extend protection to employees who work for private or public companies and who are subjected to an abusive work environment. The law makes the bully the responsible party, though companies can be held liable if they do nothing to prevent or stop the bullying. The bill also makes retaliation for the complaint actionable.

The bill recognizes how bullying affects companies' bottom lines. It reads in part that "abusive work environments have serious consequences for employers, including reduced employee productivity and morale, higher turnover, and absenteeism rates and significant increases in medical and workers' compensation claims."

For now, there is little a bullied employee can do apart from reporting the situation to HR.

"I do counsel the target to at least say 'no' one time and stand up for themselves at least one time," said Mattice.

According to Mattice, the first question HR will ask is whether the target has addressed the behavior with the other person. HR will want to see that the target has tried to work out the problems before getting involved.

"I also counsel targets to document everything that happens in a journal and if there is any tangible evidence like emails that they should collect those things," said Mattice. The journal and evidence can then be taken to HR.

"I tell them to focus just on what is happening, not what they feel about it. The journal is not meant to share emotions."

— *Lynn Bentley*

CHAPTER 24

New pressure on military hazing: Rite or wrong?

WHEN SEAN PAUL BRINSTON joined the Navy, he didn't know that he would be serving his country by piling charred human feces.

While in Afghanistan, Navy corpsman Brinston's platoon was ordered by a sergeant to tidy up a burn pit — a landfill of garbage, thrown-out food and human defecation. "All of the stuff down there is anything you can think of, and at night coyotes get down there," said Brinston, who is based at a naval medical center in Portsmouth, Va. The company reluctantly began the daunting task, an experience that Brinston now considers hazing. "We used to burn the 'wag bags' (bags of feces) at night, but some of them weren't burned that day because everyday bags get thrown down there," he said. "It smelled horrible."

In another instance, Brinston said his platoon was ordered to cover all the sand in the compound with gravel just to kill time. After about five hours of working on a 120-degree day, the commanding officer said that roughly 800 square feet was enough. Brinston and his platoon were ordered to cover the base with gravel to keep them busy. He considers this one of many ways he was hazed in the military.

The word hazing alone still gives former Army Staff Sgt. William Titus chills. "I'm not touching that with a 16-foot pole," he said.

Even 40 years after his service in the Army, including two tours in Vietnam, Titus remains tight-lipped about hazing in the military for fear of repercussions. His motto is simple:

"One man hazes as another man grazes."

Although the U.S. military doesn't report hazing statistics, there have been several media reports that indicate that hazing is still an issue. One of the most publicized incidents happened on April 3, 2011, when Marine Lance Cpl. Harry Lew committed suicide while serving in Afghanistan. Prior to his death, he had been reportedly punched and kicked in the head, ordered to do leg lifts with sandbags and had sand poured on his face, among other things. Two of the three Marines accused of hazing Lew stood trial. One was found not guilty and another accepted a plea deal for a 30-day jail sentence. The third Marine was still awaiting trial.

Following Lew's death, several members of the House of Representatives including his aunt, U.S. Rep. Judy Chu (D-Calif.), teamed up to shed light on military hazing. They wrote letters to the House Armed Services Committee and the House Oversight and Government Reform Committee, requesting that the groups hold hearings on the matter.

"The highest military officials must make eliminating hazing a top priority," said Chu, in a statement. "They must stop pretending there is no problem. None of this will change until the secretary of Defense commits to eradicate the culture of hazing that is so ingrained within our troops. Service members in positions of responsibility in the field must be made to feel that they should stop hazing when they see it, rather than encourage it, or turn the other way."

The subculture of hazing took center stage once again on Feb. 4, 2012, when the Navy reported that eight sailors aboard the USS Bonhomme Richard were discharged for strangling and beating a fellow sailor as an initiation rite that was caught on video.

Initiation rites, like line-crossing ceremonies, are customary in the Navy, Marines and Coast Guard. In a line-crossing ceremony, veteran sailors (shellbacks) initiate their shipmates who haven't crossed the Equator (pollywogs). Common practices include spraying "wogs" with fire hoses, locking them in stocks and enclosing them in coffins filled with salt water. These rituals, originally used to ensure new sailors could handle life at sea, escalated over time and have even led to deaths.

The United States isn't the only country with hazing in its military. Foreign armed forces were also found to have a number of hazing altercations, according to the U.S. Department of State's 2010 Human Rights Report [http://www.state.gov/j/drl/rls/hrrpt/2010/].

Russia's military is one of the most infamous for hazing. The country's Ministry of Defense reported 14 servicemen died from being hazed in 2010. However, the Union of Committees of Soldiers' Mothers of Russia, a human rights organization, estimates that the number of hazing deaths to be around 2,000. In 2009, the group said it received 9,523 complaints of military hazing.

"The complaints mostly concerned beatings, but also included sexual abuse, torture, and enslavement," according to the report. "Soldiers often did not report hazing to unit officers or military prosecutors due to fear of reprisals, since in some cases officers allegedly tolerated or even encouraged hazing as a means of controlling their units."

Hazing among Russian soldiers revolves around "dedovshchina," a Russian term literally translated as "rule of the grandfathers." "Ded," Russian for grandfather, refers to senior conscripts, who subject lower ranks to humiliating activities and abuse. According to military officials, abuse in the military, particularly dedovschina, increased 150 percent in the first six months of 2010 compared to 2009.

Other nations that reported military hazing include Japan, Lithuania, Kazakhstan, South Korea, Tajikistan, Turkmenistan and the Ukraine.

Although Italy's human rights report didn't mention hazing as an issue, the country's military has a term similar to dedovshchina, called "nonnismo," stemming from the word "nonno," which also means grandfather.

Brinston said that hazing could be worse in foreign militaries because in some cases there are no rules or a lack of enforcement. But even in the U.S. military, he said there's a lack of enforcement.

As of July 2005, the Navy defines hazing as "any conduct whereby a military member or members, regardless of service or rank, without proper authority causes another military member or members, regardless of service or rank, to suffer or be exposed to any activity which is cruel, abusive, humiliating, oppressive, demeaning, or harmful."

Corpsman Sean Paul Brinston, on the far left, served in Afghanistan.

Navy policy, like rules of other U.S. military branches, states that hazing will not be tolerated. Although Brinston said rules have helped, he said he still believes hazing will never be put to an end. "A lot guys don't even know they are being hazed. They come in not knowing what's right from wrong, and they're told to shut up and go with the flow."

— *Tony Briscoe*

PART 4
Social Aggression

CHAPTER 25

Bullying-suicide connection has many factors

WHEN JOURNALIST NEIL MARR and his co-author, Tim Field, coined the word "bullycide" in their 2001 book, "Bullycide: Death at Playtime," they brought the world's attention to the devastating link between bullying and suicide. Bullycide: Death at Playtime was first published in the United Kingdom but has since been published in 30 countries including the United States.

Since then, 49 states have enacted some form of anti-bullying legislation, leading schools to review, rewrite or create anti-bullying policies in hopes of preventing bullying and the devastation of suicide sometimes brought on by bullying. The word bullycide has become the accepted term to describe the bullying-related suicide of a child or young adult.

The re-release of Marr's book in February of 2011, 10 years after its original release, has prompted a re-examination of this use of bullycide to describe a suicide linked to bullying.

Suicide prevention professionals call the term bullycide misleading because it implies a direct link between the bullying and the suicide when a direct cause-and-effect link is hard to establish.

In fact, statistics show that in 2009, 13.8% of U.S. high school students reported that they had seriously considered attempting suicide during the 12 months preceding the survey; 6.3% of students reported that they had actually attempted suicide one or more times during the same period. And many of those students were not bullied. Bullying is clearly not the cause of all suicidal thoughts and many teens who are bullied do not consider suicide.

Some researchers worry that the term implies a closer and clearer relationship than can be proved.

"We prefer to not use the term 'bullycide,' said Jill Harkavy-Freidman, Ph.D., senior director of research and prevention at the American Foundation for the Prevention of Suicide. "Suicide is very complex, even within one individual. Bullying is associated with, but not causal in suicide. For someone already at risk for suicide, bullying could be a trigger."

Those risks, according to the Suicide Prevention Resource Center, include mental disorders, particularly mood disorders, anxiety disorders and certain personality disorders. alcohol and other substance use. some major physical illnesses, previous attempt at suicide, or a family history of suicide.

Two of those suicide risk factors, feelings of hopelessness and isolation, are often reported by people who have been bullied. People who bully often report those feelings, too. Bullying and suicide risk also intersect in factors such as relational or social loss and a lack of social support.

Dr. Madelyn S. Gould, professor of child and adolescent psychiatry at Columbia University in New York City, published a study in October 2011 that confirmed a strong three-way link between depression, bullying and suicide. Her study also showed that kids who are bullied and kids who bully have the same risk of suicide ideation and suicide behavior, provided that depression is also present.

"The data show that victims and their bullies are both at risk for suicide," Harkavy-Freidman said. It is important that both bullies and their victims be brought into the suicide prevention equation.

Marr agrees that the word bullycide is "grammatically ambiguous" but says that "bullycide" as a simple headline has been effective in "heightening awareness of the very real dangers" of bullying.

"Perhaps the greatest feedback I've had from the book is from bereaved parents who no longer feel alone in their grief, understanding that other people's children have been bullied to death without them or so-called 'responsible authorities' having spotted the red flags," Marr said.

It is precisely those red flags that suicide prevention professionals would like educators, parents and doctors to look for.

Harkavy-Friedman stresses that parents and educators need to have a deep knowledge of the child to see the signs of distress: changes in behavior, changes in sleeping or eating patterns, mood swings or a constant flatness, and especially, social isolation. If the signs are there, talk about them with the child.

"Let them know you are on their side so that they feel respected and not judged," said Harkavy-Friedman. "And if they can't talk to you, encourage them to talk to somebody."

— *Lynn Bentley*

CHAPTER 26

Relaxed taboo means more suicide news

THE CONNECTION BETWEEN BULLYING and suicide is elusive, but news coverage of suicide is visibly becoming more acceptable.

Erosion of the old taboo leads to increased coverage of suicides and the natural impression that suicides themselves must be increasing.

According to reports from the Centers for Disease Control and Prevention, a decline in youth suicide rates from 1990 to 2003 was followed by a rise in 2004. From 1999 to 2009, attempts by students in grades 9–12 requiring medical attention decreased 26.9%.

However, suicide news has become more frequent and prominent as newsrooms relax what had been a largely unwritten rule against covering suicides.

The Hastings Star Gazette in Minnesota described its policy change in January, 2012.

The newspaper told readers, "Essentially, we were sweeping the problem under the rug."

"This week we changed that policy. We will write about mental health issues in the police report … It's a significant use of police resources, and the public ought to know how their department is spending its time. . . .

"The greater good in this, we hope, is that by telling you about these instances you'll see how prevalent it is. You will have greater awareness about the ongoing struggles taking place in your community. Once you are armed with that information, we hope you'll do what you can to help your fellow residents."

The Star Gazette is not alone in relaxing this taboo.

In September, 2011, Toronto Star Public Editor Kathy English wrote, "If journalism's first obligation is to tell the truth, why has the truth that some desperate people take their own lives been largely off-limits to journalists? For many years, the Star's policy has been not to reveal that someone committed suicide unless there is some overriding public interest in doing so."

English described her early years learning the craft as a reporter and how she accepted the unwritten code of the newsroom to keep most suicides out of print.

She cited a 2010 article by Liam Casey, then an intern for the Ottawa Citizen, who now works with her at the Star.

Casey had written wrote about his first encounter with this journalistic taboo during his internship. His article in the Ryerson Review of Journalism included an unusual appeal: "I contemplated killing myself five years ago. Now, to help others, I call on all journalists to break the silence on our final taboo."

Casey described how police, not journalists, had told him about the unwritten rule: "The newsroom buzzes when I arrive, or maybe that's just my heart, fluttering away. (The assignment editor) tells me to follow up with police. About an hour later, the cops say he was a 'jumper,' but that's just for my information since, the officer tells me, the paper doesn't report suicides."

Casey wrote that his editors "tell me not to pursue it further. I move on to a story about a man trying to lure a child into his van near a public school. At least it means I can avoid writing about suicide.

"But I am confused, ignorant of the accepted practice of not reporting suicides."

Casey added, "Suicide avoidance is a throwback to journalism's dark days, a time when editors and news producers could choose to ignore unpleasant matters."

The Dart Center for Journalism & Trauma helps journalists cover suicide, bullying and other issues.

In an article for Dart about teen suicides, Brian Slodysko wrote, "Many newspapers and media outlets have policies against covering the suicides of young people, especially if the death involves a minor.

"Though it's a daunting task, and some editors are reluctant to cover suicide, does this mean the issue should be avoided by student journalists?"

"Not necessarily."

Slodysko argued in favor of reporting that runs down rumors, reveals social service needs and reports resources.

Newsrooms typically do not have policy manuals on news judgment. Sometimes, a newsroom will have a stylebook that dictates writing style and might include a few policies.

The Detroit Free Press stylebook of 1989 said, "We try to honor family requests that suicide not be identified as the cause of death in obituaries. Circumstances that put a self-inflicted death in the public eye, however, might merit its mention in a news story and elsewhere."

The guideline did not appear in a 1992 revision of the stylebook, but the old taboo lingered.

Besides the obvious issues of sensitivity and discomfort, journalists minimized suicide coverage out of concerns about "suicide contagion" — copycat suicides.

In a 2008 article for the Poynter Institute, a school for journalists, veteran TV newsman Al Tompkins began by saying flat out, "Journalists usually avoid suicide stories." He then listed coverage guidelines from the American Association of Suicidology.

Three years later, Tompkins wrote about how Tampa's lead TV station had started the evening news with the story of a 10-year-old who had died by suicide.

Tompkins did a video deconstruction of how the station told the story and concluded with "The one thing that would be worse than losing a young life is to lose it and learn nothing from that loss."

Restrained coverage of suicide was consistent with limited news about mental illness, sexual assault and AIDS. In each of those areas, the pendulum has swung toward greater disclosure.

In 2001, several U.S. health agencies issued guidelines for media coverage of suicide.. The guidelines advised against prominent placement of the story and descriptions or photographs of suicide methods.

The guidelines also recommended that journalists avoid the phrases like "commit suicide," "failed attempt" and "doing it for attention."

A study by the U.S. National Institutes for Health of suicide coverage in 2002 and 2003 concluded, "Newspaper suicide stories from 2002 and 2003 did not show consistent adherence to the 2001 media guidelines . . . Of particular concern is the absence of helpful suicide prevention information and resources, and the large number of stories that gave detailed information about suicide method and location. A positive trend was that very few suicide stories were on the front page."

A relaxation of taboos against suicide coverage in some newsrooms would work against that trend.

RESOURCES

A Tormenting Problem: An Exploration of New-Age Bullying, The Dart Center, 2011 [http://dartcenter.org/content/tormenting-problem-exploration-new-age-bullying-2]

The Power of a Bully, The Dart Center, 2010 [http://dartcenter.org/content/power-bully]

Roanoke Times policy on suicide coverage, Roanoke Times, 2009 [http://www.roanoke.com/newsservices/wb/xp-59614#31]

Suicide coverage always challenging by Therese Bottomly, The Oregonian, 2007 [http://blog.oregonlive.com/oregonianeditors/2007/06/_more_than_500_oregonians.html]

Covering Teen Suicide: One Paper's Decision by Barbara Walsh, The Poynter Institute, 2005.

[http://www.poynter.org/uncategorized/36012/covering-teen-suicide-one-papers-decision/]

— *Joe Grimm*

CHAPTER 27

School rampages defy easy explanation

SINCE THE 1999 SCHOOL shooting at Columbine High School in Littleton, Colo., parents, educators and government officials have been worried about a link between bullying and school shootings.

Before killing themselves in the school library, Eric Harris and Dylan Klebold shot and killed 11 students, one teacher and wounded 23 others. Bombs the two had planted in the cafeteria and their cars did not go off.

Initial reports on the Columbine shooting indicated that the shootings might be retaliation for the two boys having been bullied. People feared that there was a connection between bullying, school massacres and suicide, Columbine changed the way many people treat bullying. In Georgia, those fears soon led to the passage of anti-bullying legislation. All but one state have since followed. Bill Belsey, the Canadian educator who created cyber-bulling.ca and www.bullying.org, said that Columbine helped motivate him to be an anti-bullying activist.

However, after reviewing journals, videos and other evidence, psychologists, law enforcement officials and other experts have concluded that the shootings were the actions of individuals with personality disorders.

Dr. Peter Langman, an expert on the psychology of youths who commit rampage school shootings, concurs. In his book, "Why Kids Kill: In The Minds Of School Shooters," Langman describes three types of school shooter: psychopathic (Harris), psychotic (Klebold) and traumatized.

Traumatized shooters experience unstable home lives and multiple forms of abuse. Mitchell Johnson, for example, came from an unstable home life in which his father was an abusive alcoholic. From the age of 8, Mitchell was sexually abused by an older boy. In 1999, Mitchell and his friend, 11-year-old Andrew Golden, shot and killed four students, one teacher and wounded 10 others at Westside Middle School in Arkansas.

Langman recently studied 35 school shooters, including Harris, Klebold and Johnson, but found that only two had killed someone who had actually picked on them. "Teasing (or bullying) may have been a significant factor in a few shootings, but the idea that the shootings are retaliation against bullies is usually wrong," Langman said.

According to the Centers for Disease Control and Prevention, 19.9 percent (or 3,400,000 students) in grades nine through 12 reported incidents of bullying in 2009, yet The National School Safety Center's Report on School Associated Violent Deaths for that same period details only eight fatal incidents.

In trying to understand the motives of a school-associated shooting, people will often ask if the shooter had ever been bullied. "The answer would be yes for most students in the country," said Langman, "but almost none of them will ever commit mass murder."

It is clear that bullying is a major problem in U.S., schools but it is not the significant factor in school-associated fatalities. Schizophrenia and depression often become overt in adolescence, according to Dr. Frank Ochberg, clinical professor of psychiatry at Michigan State University and former associate director of the National Institute of Mental Health. These forms of mental illness are more frequently dangerous to the individuals who suffer from them but when these illnesses become lethal to others, as happened at Virginia Tech, we need better answers.

Ochberg, who was one of the experts who worked on the Columbine shooting, also believes that it is the access that these seriously ill kids have to guns that is the significant factor in American school shootings.

"If kids could not and did not bring guns to school, we wouldn't have Columbine, Virginia Tech or Chardon, Ohio," he wrote for CNN.

— *Lynn Bentley*

CHAPTER 28

Bullies in the cinema

THE DOCUMENTARY "BULLY" CHALLENGES relationships, just as school bullying does.

After an advance screening of the film in Birmingham, Mich., parents, school administrators and children had a strained but civil exchange.

One mother told a school superintendent that schools had done nothing to stop the bullying of her daughter, who watched the film with her. Seventh grader Ethan Wolf and his father, Richard, participating on a panel, accused schools of inaction. Ethan Wolf said he has been bullied.

Greater parental involvement by parents of bullies and their targets keeps coming up the documentary and resonated in the community discussion afterward.

When one mother asked how she could know what was going on with her child and social media, someone called out, "Parenting."

The documentary follows several students as they are bullied by classmates. Very little of the action takes place in classrooms. The bullying it shows happens at the bus stop, in hallways, the gym, at lunch, on the playground and, most violently, on the bus.

The National Center for Education statistics reports that students say that bullying hotspots are hallways, locker room and buses. With teachers monitoring classrooms, bullying goes underground.

"Bully" deals very little with cyberbullying and the politics of social exclusion, focusing instead on verbal and physical bullying, which makes for better video.

Scan this code with a QR-reader to see the trailer, or go to http://www.youtube.com/watch?v=W1g9RV9OKhg.

In Bully, students' most revealing moments are in their safe zones, at home. They are not always forthcoming. They bury it. One of the panelists at the screening, Det. Sgt. Dannen Ofeara of the Oakland County Sheriff's Dept. said that bullied students have "a thousand-mile stare," when he interviews them. They have bottled up their emotions.

In the movie, one student says that a good week is when nothing bad happens. The filmmakers, concerned about the escalating violence they were capturing on the school bus, showed it to his parents. His frustrated mother asked why he wasn't talking about this and whether being bullied made him feel good. He said, "I'm starting to think I don't feel anything anymore."

The documentary initially challenged the relationship among parents and teachers. Neither group comes off well in the film. The world that kids live in — on the bus, at gym, at lunch — is largely invisible to them.

In "Bully," one girl says bullying drove her to take a gun onto the school bus to make the bullying stop. An officer in the film said she faced more than 40 felony charges for kidnapping and threatening the other kids on the bus.

The film and especially the conversation after the screening challenged the relationship and role of bystanders. There seemed to be consensus, and perhaps a growing national feeling, that it is no longer OK to stand by and watch others get bullied. Once innocent bystanders, the observers are being pushed to get involved and to change their environments.

The Motion Picture Association of America initially gave "Bully" an R rating because the F-word is dropped six times, by students, usually at the bus stop or on the bus. The rating would have meant that children under 17 would not be admitted to the film without a parent or guardian.

Director-producer Lee Hirsch was adamant about keeping the F-bombs in the movie. The rating was changed under the pressure of half a million online signatures in a campaign started by the 17-year-old target of school bullying in Michigan, Katy Butler. She wanted the rating changed to PG-13 so that its intended audience would be admitted to the movie by themselves..

Many students under 17 attended the screening with their parents. One mother in line with her 14-year-old son showed the email she had received from his middle school principal offering free tickets.

On the way out of the theater, a mother told her daughter, "If someone were to talk to you like that, I hope you would come have a talk with me."

— *Joe Grimm*

CHAPTER 29

Bullies and targets are sometimes the same person

IT SEEMS THE TWO would have nothing in common. There is the bully, and then the target waiting for the next attack. It turns out, though, that the two might share similarities.

In fact, they might be the same person. According to a survey by the Journal of Early Adolescence, almost half of 4,260 children who admitted in the study to bullying also claimed they had been targets of bullying.

"More than half of bullies are bullied at home," said Glenn R. Stutzky, a clinical instructor on the Michigan State University School of Social Work. "They've been a victim at home, whether it be from parents or siblings, and do what they have to do so they aren't put in a spot to be a victim."

Stutzky said that bully targets need serious help, and leaving them untreated can lead to more violence.

"For the child who's been targeted by a bully, their life is a living hell," said Stutzky. "Bullying is probably the most frequently occurring form of violence in American schools today and it's really the engine that's driving the majority of violence. It's a huge problem."

Due to the similarities between the emotional make-up of bullies and targets, the bullying cycle is hard to break.

"It all comes down to having control over the other person," said Larry Schiamberg, Michigan State University Human Development and Family Studies professor. "Bullies can easily become victims and victims can easily become bullies. It's important to encourage kids to report bullying in order to help break the cycle."

Schiamberg said that because bullying is a continuity of a behavior, the cycle seems to continue. "This is not simply one nasty comment. This is not simply one, maybe abrupt push. This is not simply one behavior. This is behaviors repeated over time," he said.

One of the main principles that make the target and bully alike is the fact that they have poor problem-solving skills within social situations. This creates a situation where neither can resolve the situation. Without a resolution, the cycle continues.

"Typical bullies and victims both have negative attitudes toward others, feel badly about themselves and most likely grow up in a home with conflict," said Christie Nicholson, Scientific American community editor. "Due to these similarities, it is easy for children to go back and forth from being bullies and bully victims."

Bully-victims, students who are bullied and who bully, tend to lack emotional control. Their lack of control may result in them reacting very emotionally toward teasing and in return, losing control of their retaliatory aggression. One of the dividing characteristic that makes some bullies and targets different, according to the journal "School Psychology Quarterly," is that bullies tend to dislike school more than those who become their targets.

"It all comes down to children who are bullies, bullied or both sharing similar outlooks and similar difficulties with their environment," Nicholson said. "That is why there always is a cycle between bullies and victims that seems to go back and forth."

— *Colby Berthume*

PART 5
Solutions

CHAPTER 30

Hospital's new center takes a medical approach

MICHIGAN WAS THE 48TH state to pass anti-bullying legislation, but it may be one of the first to develop clinical treatment for those affected by bullying.

William Beaumont Hospital in Royal Oak is expected to open a clinic to help victims of bullying, bullies, bystanders and families on May 4, 2012. Anti-bullying activist Kevin Epling said a medical approach is on the cutting edge of bullying therapy. "I've not heard of anything like this taking place in a hospital," said Epling. "Most of these are providers that parents would have to find, such as counselors or someone at the general community health office."

Dr. Marlene Seltzer, director of the No Bullying Live Empowered (NoBLE) Center, struck upon the idea while practicing gynecology over the years. "I've always been interested in the psycho-socio issues of medicine like domestic violence, and gynecology has a lot of those types of issues," said Seltzer, who's been an OB/GYN for nearly 16 years. "It wasn't so far to go from domestic violence to bullying as an area of interest."

Depression, anxiety, low self-esteem,

Marlene Seltzer: The idea came from patients.
. Photo by J.T. Bohland.

stomachaches, headaches, insomnia, bedwetting and suicide are all potential consequences of bullying, Seltzer said. After hearing of a Florida teen being videotaped as she was bullied by several classmates, Seltzer had to get involved.

"For some reason, that really struck a chord with me that we've gotten to a point in our society where kids beat each other up and post it on YouTube, and we are all just OK with that," she said. "That put me on the path toward trying to do something about this issue."

She contacted Alonzo Lewis, Beaumont Children's Hospital's vice president of women's and children's services, to discuss a solution. "Wow, wouldn't this be a neat project for us to launch," recalled Lewis on his initial meeting with Seltzer. "(NoBLE) would bring some new patient volume to Beaumont and service a need that doesn't have enough support in the community."

Originally, Seltzer planned to combat bullying through a hotline, but she quickly realized that wasn't enough. She said the NoBLE Center's main goal will be to provide mental health services to youth impacted by bullying. However, Seltzer said the center will not directly prescribe medication.

Alonzo Lewis: Looking to provide a needed service. Photo by J.T. Bohland.

Community outreach will be another vital area if the center is to meet its full potential.

"Beaumont already has relationships with schools in the area and so we'll use those already established relationships to go face to face and meet with superintendents, principals, counselors and teachers to really explain the program and answer any questions they have," said Seltzer. "So when they refer students, they're referring them to something they're familiar with."

Lewis said that after hearing Seltzer propose the concept for the center, funding became the biggest concern. But thanks to the hospital's support and several donations, NoBLE had secured $350,000 as of March 30.

"So far, we've been very lucky to receive funds from the Children's Miracle Network and also from Beaumont Children's hospital," said Seltzer. "We've had a private family foundation donate some money and we're about to embark on a fundraising campaign. What we're hoping is that this issue has unfortunately touched so many people's lives but that people will want to do something and support us."

The NoBLE Center, which will be on campus in the medical office building, is starting small, with four mental health providers plus Seltzer. Although the project is in the early stages of development, Lewis said he's confident about its potential.

"Beaumont Hospital is a leader in cardiovascular medicine, robotic surgery, transplant surgery . . . So, we're a leader in all these sophisticated medical programs, and this type of program positions us to be a leader, as well. I have no doubt that as soon as our program grows we're going to get calls from all over the country in terms of 'How did you make this happen?' and 'Can we use your model to develop a program or service in our state?'"

— *Tony Briscoe and J.T. Bohland*

CHAPTER 31

Celebrities use their stages to denounce bullying

"BABY, I WAS BORN this way" is a lyric in Lady Gaga's hit song, "Born This Way." The song highlights what it means to be different and how it should be less of a faux pas and more of a norm. A growing number of celebrities have started speaking out about how they were picked on as children and to speak up for people who are bullied today.

"There are many celebrities that are now openly talking about their own bouts with bullying. It is the popular topic," said Bully Police USA Co-Director Kevin Epling.

Celebrities ranging from Lady Gaga to former President Bill Clinton to television talk show host Ellen Degeneres are all candidly opening up about their bullying experiences. Degeneres has used her television program to warn that "teenage bullying and teasing is an epidemic in this country."

Referencing the death of former Rutgers student, Tyler Clementi, who was bullied and later took his own life, Degeneres shared her own story of bullying in an emotionally charged video message. Epling said Degeneres "is also talking about the topic and not just when the media is reporting a story. She is trying to keep it in the public eye when she can."

E-Poll, a market research company, conducted a study that found that "During teens' growth process, they often rely on celebrities and images in popular culture to act as connectors to social acceptance, but also to help them define their own identity."

Another way that celebrities are waging anti-bullying efforts is through their areas of expertise, as the band Foster the People does with its music. Some of the band's most popular songs have anti-bullying undertones, which has led group leader Mark Foster to be more vocal on the issue.

In a CNN interview, Foster spoke of his struggle with bullying while growing up.

"I experienced bullying a lot," he said, "I was kind of a small kid with a big mouth, and so I always got myself in trouble . . . And I grew up in Cleveland. It's pretty blue collar, and kids know how to fight there, so that was a real thing, for sure." He spoke about the band's most popular and award winning song, "Pumped Up Kicks," about the internal struggle of an adolescent and the prospect of what to do with a gun.

The lyrics in Foster the People's song "Don't Stop (Color on the Walls)" paints the picture of young children dealing with bullying and, as Foster said, is something he has dealt with himself.

> "One, two, three, close your eyes and count to four
> I'm gonna (I'd like) to hide behind my bedroom door
> Crayons on walls
> I'll color on them all
> I'll draw until I've broken every law."

Although celebrities are able to capture the attention of large audiences when they speak, Epling says he is cautious about accepting their support.

"There is a part of me that, until I really see what they are actually doing, I am wary of celebrities jumping on the bandwagon," Epling said.

Celebrities often ride popular issues, and bullying has become one of those topics. Lady Gaga's foundation says it hopes to, "lead youth into a braver new society where each individual is accepted and loved as the person they were born to be."

This is the type of message that Epling and other parents of those affected by bullying want to hear.

— *Seth Beifel*

CHAPTER 32

Authors anticipated rising interest in subject

VAMPIRES AND WIZARDS ARE not the only subjects sweeping the youth literature market in recent years. By looking beyond those titles to "Dear Bully," "Hate List" and "Payback," one sees that books about bullying have flushed the market over the past several years. And it wasn't in response to the media attention on the subject.

Nicole DuFort is a district sales and marketing manager for Random House, the world's largest publisher of books for young readers. "The initiative to publish literature with bullying themes doesn't come from the publishers or editors, she said. "It's the authors who anticipated the national conversation and wrote about it."

Manuscripts usually take one to two years before becoming published, said DuFort.

One such author is A.S. King, who wrote "Everybody Sees the Ants." "Ants" is the story of Lucky Lindeman, a high school student who endures extensive bullying at the hands of a classmate while he dreams of a grandfather he never knew.

In her blog [http://www.as-king.info], she speaks about what led her to the theme.

"When I wrote "Ants," bullying was not a hot topic," she said. "In fact, I was asked by one editor to take the bullying out of the book. Books take quite a while to go from my computer to the shelf. What's a hot topic today is not going to be a hot topic in three years. And long after this hot topic goes away and is replaced with another, those million a week will be suffering in silence, just like they/we always did."

Books like King's are being recognized for the solace they can give bullied youth and their parents.

The Young Adult Library Services Association is a division of the American Library Association. Each year, it compiles lists of themed books that libraries and schools can use on certain subjects. For 2012, a Sticks and Stones [http://www.ala.org/yalsa/booklists/poppaper/2012#sticks] list was born, highlighting 24 examples of youth literature that focuses on bullying.

Valerie Davis is a librarian in the Campbell County Public Library system in Newport, Ky., and she served as chair of the Young Adult Library Services Association selection committee this year. Her library is directly across the street from a high school and, as she says, she sees the good and bad in teenage life.

"As I find with many books about tough subjects, rarely do you get a teenager coming in and saying, 'I need a book about (bullying')," she said. "But by creating the list and the resource, we are sliding a book into someone else's hand."

In her position, Davis conducts literature trainings for teachers across Ohio, Kentucky and Indiana. It's at these times that she would share books that could be added to teachers' existing or new curricula focusing on bullying.

Anne Nuttall teaches sixth grade at Crivitz Public Schools in Crivitz, Wisc. Over the past year, she's seen both bullying and reports of bullying go up among her students. Despite discussions about what bullying actually is and sharing the district policy with her students and their parents, questions still arise.

"If there are resources available to teachers," she said, "I would definitely utilize them. Books about bullying would be a great addition to my classroom, with students that may be identified as bullies seeing what it's like for the kids they may pick on. And the kids who get picked on would simply see that they're not alone."

— Dustin Petty

How one district uses the classics to fight bullying

English teachers Stephanie Livingston and Sue Doneson in Michigan's Haslett High School approach bullying in school by integrating novels that deal with respect and responsibility into the 9 to 12 grade English language arts curriculum.

They hope students will discuss certain novels in a safe classroom environment and that these dialogues about characters will influence daily lives.

Students in ninth grade read "Speak" by Laurie Halse Anderson and "The Glass Castle" by Jeanette Walls.

"In the books, students see coping strategies and ways to deal with the bullying and ostracism. Both of these pieces have to deal with young people. 'Speak' is about a ninth grade girl, so that very much connects with their experiences," said Livingston.

"In the English 10 course, we teach 'Of Mice and Men' by John Steinbeck and we talk quite a bit about overcoming prejudice toward those with disabilities and the choices we make to survive that prejudice, specifically related to a character with disabilities," said Doneson. "In the honors section, we teach classics 'Scarlet Letter' and 'To Kill A Mockingbird,' both dealing with ostracism from a community and how a person overcomes that and the dehumanizing treatment a person can overcome if they are considered an outsider from that community."

Students in the 11th grade read "The Lord of the Flies" by William Golding.

"We talk quite a bit about the dehumanizing treatment of one group of boys toward another and the physical size difference and how that plays into bullying and harassment and how that is used as a mechanism to intimidate. We talk about coping mechanisms and ways in which the group dynamic can change and be altered with particular leaders and how to deal with that," said Livingston.

The 12th grade world literature course is geared toward recognizing the importance of personal responsibility and respecting diverse cultures.

School Board Trustee Robert Fowler said, "We've been doing this for a long time — there's so much attention to bullying these days, as if we've just woken up and realized that it's a bad thing. I actually think that some of our legislators think that if they hadn't passed this law, nobody would do anything about bullying and that's not the case with our district."

— *Adam Ilenich*

CHAPTER 33

The children's television channel Cartoon Network turned up its stand against bullying in 2011 and early 2012.

IT STARTED WITH A definition. According to the Cartoon Network website, bullying is "when someone repeatedly hurts or threatens another person on purpose. Bullying comes in many forms. And it can happen in person, in writing, online, on cellphones, in school, on the bus, at home, anywhere." The last part of the definition is the most important: "Wherever it happens, it's **not** acceptable."

During the fall of 2011, Cartoon Network created a campaign to promote bullying awareness. It started with a few commercials starring the cast of the show "Dude, What Would Happen." They present a situation where a newcomer is bullied by another child, and an innocent bystander runs to an adult for help. At the end of the commercial, they say bullying is wrong and if you see something, say something.

A few months later, the network began airing more anti-bullying commercials. They featured cartoon characters, actors from various shows and celebrities who have been bullied, all joining the Stop Bullying, Speak Up initiative. Programming suddenly switched from the "Dude" commercial to a huge variety, with anti-bullying announcements being played almost every commercial break.

On March 11, 2012, Cartoon Network aired a half-hour special titled "Speak Up." The special included stories from celebrities such as former NBA player Chris Webber, tennis player Serena Williams and President Barack Obama, and testimonials from real-life victims of bullying. The program was designed to create discussion, especially within families and schools, about bullying.

The program was candid. The network warned that some of the language was vulgar and could make some people uncomfortable. Kevin, a bullying victim, talked about starving himself for a summer because other children were calling him fat. Another child, Aaron, said he was bullied in grade school and his grades suffered as a result of constant teasing. Jackson Rogow, co-star of "Dude, What Would Happen," said that being bullied as a child turned him into a bully as he got older.

The program also discussed solutions to bullying. One solution is communication, as victims are encouraged to talk about the incidents with someone and to seek help. Bystanders and witnesses were encouraged to stand up for the victims and to get help.

One segment featured Alye Pollack, who made a YouTube video in 2011, called "Words Do Hurt," about being bullied. She talked about how her bullies saw the video and apologized after watching it. According to Pollack, people even began sticking up for her and others after she posted the video. Some bullying targets who saw her video were inspired to make their own. One year after posting, in March 2012, she posted another video, "Words Do Hurt: 1 Year Later." She encouraged other victims to hang in there. The video also includes links to the suicide prevention hotline [http://www.sprc.org/].

Cartoon Network also has a website dedicated to anti-bullying [http://www.cartoonnetwork.com/promos/stopbullying/]. There are games and literature for children, a page for parents dealing with bullied children and even a page for teachers on how to deal with incidents of bullying in school. There's also a link to the website of author Rosalind Wiseman, who answers viewer questions about bullying via a video blog.

For more information, visit www.StopBullyingSpeakUp.com [http://www.cartoonnetwork.com/tv_shows/promotion_landing_page/stopbullying/index.html].

— *Devyne Lloyd*

CHAPTER 34

Questionnaires get at what happens and how often

IN TODAY'S WORLD, SCHOOLS must intervene to stop bullying. How do they know if their programs are successful?

Schools sometimes turn to questionnaires that are filled out by students and given to educators. They use the students' answers to better understand how they view bullying, who is being bullied and if those views change throughout the programs implemented.

"Bullying surveys are used to measure the prevalence of bullying and to guide intervention efforts," said Dewey Cornell, clinical psychologist and professor of education at the University of Virginia. "They allow schools to gauge whether their intervention efforts are being successful. Ideally, they are carefully developed with extensive research to establish their reliability and validity."

Ken Rigby, adjunct professor at the University of South Australia, said questions that allow students to describe their feelings are usually best in raising awareness. Rigby also said that questionnaires better equip teachers to deal with bullying and can get parents to be more involved.

Not all surveys are developed carefully, Cornell said.

"Unfortunately, anyone can make up a survey that may have little reliability or validity," he said. With good surveys, administrators can get an honest look at who is being bullied and how the students view bullying. Schools may purchase surveys and other materials at both websites listed above and can also have school counselors create them.

Delaware's program, called "No Bullying Allowed," was implemented by the state's Department of Justice. A key ingredient of the program is the bully questionnaire that is provided to schools as a tool. "The forms were created from the Olweus project," DDJ Ombudsman and school crimes investigator Joseph Flinn said. "The project was funded through a grant we received through the state."

Initially called a "bully-proofing" program in the late 1990s, it has evolved into a tiered approach to school bullying and prevention.

There are four core principles of the project that offer tips to prevent bullying in school and the classroom. One major component is understanding the importance of adult involvement. "This is where the survey is important," said Flinn. "The anonymous survey among students is used to present faculty and parents with important information."

According to a study by the Delaware Department of Justice, most bullying occurs during breaks. Because of this, the program recommends schools provide adequate supervision during recess periods along with providing teachers with a system for exchanging information about bullying that occurs during these times.

"The supervision, along with providing education and examples of what bullying is helps deter children from bullying," Flinn said. "We believe that follow-up questions in class teach students what bullying really is."

The final principle of the project calls for talks with targets, bullies, and their parents. To help with discussions, the department developed a worksheet for victims of bullying to help them think about strategies for dealing with the bully and a bully package for use after a bullying incident.

Flinn said that for the program to reach its potential, adults must commit to change the reality of bullying. He also said that they must use the resources provided by the state to show students that bullying is not acceptable.

"The goal of our program is to promote the necessary components of a healthy school climate," Flinn said. "Because our program provides an effective evaluation process, along with resources designed to provide a safe and supportive environment, our goal is accomplished."

— *Alethia Kasben and Colby Berthume*

Delaware Bully Questionnaire

Used with permission from the Delaware Department of Justice.

KIDS' QUESTIONNAIRE

Delaware Bullying Questionnaire: Before answering these questions, please be sure that you read and understand the definition of bullying. Teachers may need to read the definitions and questions to younger students.

Definition:

Ages 12 to 17, read this:

Bullying means when one person, or a group of persons, targets another person with repeated direct or indirect negative actions over a period of time which are harmful to the target either emotionally or physically. A negative action occurs when a person knowingly inflicts, or attempts to inflict, physical or emotional injury or discomfort upon another person.

Under 12, read this:

Bullying is when one child, or a group of children, keeps hurting another child with words or actions. Bullying may be hitting, shoving, kicking, name calling; playing dirty tricks, leaving out a child, spreading rumors or doing other mean things.

Bullying often, though not always, happens between students who are not friends. Sometimes bullying can happen just one time. Bullying happens when one person who has more physical or emotional power targets another person who has trouble defending himself or herself. Usually the person targeted becomes very upset.

Directions: Answer all the questions. Think about each question carefully. Fill in the blanks or circle the correct answer. Do NOT put your name on this survey.

The complete survey can be found at http://attorneygeneral. delaware.gov/schools/bullquesti.shtml.

CHAPTER 35

Suicides spurred global anti-bullying strategy

DAN OLWEUS, A PSYCHOLOGY professor in Norway, is often cited as the first major researcher of bullying. Olweus began thoroughly researching the subject in the early 1980's following the suicides of three boys aged 10 to 14, all three were potentially consequences of bullying in school.

After these suicides, Olweus went to work to prevent bullying. According to the program's website, the program led to a reduction of 50 percent or more in student reports of bullying in Norway. The report also provided evidence for marked reductions in student reports of general antisocial behavior, such as vandalism, fighting, theft and truancy.

Following such success in Norway, the Olweus Bully Prevention Program has been implemented elsewhere. In 1999, after the killings at a school in Columbine, Colo., the U.S. Department of Justice selected the program as a model for its national violence prevention strategy.

In March 2012, a South Korean film crew visited a New Jersey school district to document the effectiveness of the Olweus Program in the United States.

The news account of the visit showed how cultures were learning from one another to curb a worldwide bullying epidemic. Yeji Shin, a film producer from Korea, said in a published report that she had made the trip to America to help show how bullying could be stopped in her country.

"There are a lot of concerns right now regarding men, boys and bullying. The bullying issue is one of the worst in the world in Korea," Shin said. "We just want to show the Korean society what's out there. I definitely think, just by what we've filmed so far, we have more than enough information to bring back. This is a very rich and action-oriented program. I hope we can prove that bullying is an issue that can be managed."

In Michigan, school districts began forming or re-evaluating school policies following the anti-bullying law that was passed in December 2011. Williamston School District, which is about 10 miles east of the state's capitol, set out to define bullying and used guidelines in the Olweus Prevention Program.

Defining bullying has been very difficult for lawmakers and teachers alike, but the Williamston district defined it as "any gesture or written, verbal, graphic, or physical act (including electronically transmitted acts, i.e. internet, telephone or cell phone, personal digital assistant (PDA), or wireless handheld device) that, without regard to its subject matter or motivating animus, is intended or that a reasonable person would know is likely to harm one or more students."

The policy draft goes on to describe ways in which the school district will work to curtail bullying, many of which are similar to the Olweus program.

— *Tommy Franz*

CHAPTER 36

The power of 100

DAVID SIMANCEK, AN ASSISTANT principal who saw a student bullied in the hallway at Swartz Creek High School in Swartz Creek, Mich., believes bullying can be stopped only through a community effort by interested, willing parties.

Simancek is the mind behind the Power of 100, a group of students and staff that have united to dissolve bullying at Swartz Creek High School. As of March 2012, Simancek said more than 300 of the school's approximately 1,200 students have been to a meeting to learn about the initiative if not become involved in its campaign.

David Simancek has turned the inside and outside of his school into an anti-bullying billboard. Photo by Joe Grimm.

The initiative started in 2010 with a few students and staff who wanted to stand up for bullied students. Simancek said he saw a student in the hallway who had been bullied, and then another group of students stepped in to help. Soon Simancek was posting mysterious signs and posters around the school to get students' attention. People were intrigued to discover what the fuss was all about. Slowly, attendance at meetings began rising.

The campaign has spread to more than a quarter of the students in the school. Simancek also said he has seen many students wearing Power of 100 T-shirts.

Often, when adults try to solve bullying, they say it is just kids being kids, according to anti-bullying activist Kevin Epling. Some say bullying is a test of character.

But Epling said anti-bullying has to become normalized in school settings, with school administrators coming up with ways to report bullying. Students need to be involved in anti-bullying efforts from the beginning, he said, which Simancek said is the cornerstone of Power of 100.

Simancek also recognizes that Power of 100 is a unique program because of the willingness of its members to get along. He said the scare tactics of traditional teachers — telling students not to bully or they will be disciplined — does not discourage bullying; it only adds to the problem.

"Everyone knows it's a problem; everyone wants it to stop," he said.

— *Rachel Jackson*

CHAPTER 37

Bully policy and programs

WITH EACH NEW TRAGEDY, schools react by looking for ways to raise awareness and combat bullying. Some schools implement new policy while others wonder if that is the most effective action.

Many schools are getting results with school-run programs.

One such program is K.A.R.M.A, an initiative founded by Jessica Brookshire, a contestant in the 2009 Miss Alabama pageant. K.A.R.M.A stands for Kids Against Ridicule, Meanness and Aggression. Brookshire says that her program began as a grassroots effort in Alabama schools and it is now her "dream that one day we will see a generation of children who encourage and help one another rather than tear each other down with words."

Part of the program includes Brookshire educating students on how to "stand S.T.R.O.N.G." against bullies. Participants sign a pledge card stating that they will take action if they see bullying. S.T.R.O.N.G stands for:

Say something.

Tell an adult.

Respect the feelings of others.

Offer a helping hand if you see someone in need.

Never use your words to hurt others.

Give your best every day.

For some schools, bringing in outside programs may be too costly, but many teacher education publications are now bringing up bullying issues and solutions.

Steve Hudock, a sixth and seventh grade teacher from North Middle School in Belleville, Mich., says, "Administrators sometimes provided supplementary reading, discussions at faculty meetings and support through the office by allowing students to be referred to a counselor or administrator." He adds, "Our middle school has used a variety of approaches but hasn't been consistent with any one activity or process for handling bullying. By training all students to react to bullies and not tolerate the behavior, we can begin to change attitude and not tolerate the behavior."

One example of the supplementary reading material is Teaching Tolerance, a magazine devoted to support for teachers who care about diversity, equal opportunity and respect in their classrooms. The magazine has published a wealth of information for teachers as well as age-appropriate material like quizzes, videos and tips for use in the classroom.

Dr. Dan Olweus, whose bullying prevention program is used around the world, has written that "it is a prevalent problem in most schools that must be addressed in a systematic way." He said his program "is a comprehensive schoolwide program to prevent and reduce bullying behavior in schools. It works at four levels, the school level, the classroom level, the individual level and also the community level."

The key to having an effective anti-bullying program is to engage students and keep them active in stopping bullying. When students feel invested in a program, as opposed to feeling required to follow it because of rules, they are more likely to take action.

— *Leslie Tilson*

CHAPTER 38

"It Gets Better" campaign promises brighter futures

BILLY LUCAS, A FRESHMAN at Greenburg High School in Indiana, hanged himself in his grandmother's barn after being taunted by classmates. Friends and family of the 15-year-old said he was bullied because he was perceived to be gay.

Lucas was one of at least 34 American students to take their own lives in 2010 after dealing with an instance of bullying.

When Dan Savage, a syndicated advice columnist and blogger, read about Lucas' suicide and the suicides of other young people who were bullied for being lesbian, gay, bisexual, transgender, queer (LGBTQ) or because others believed they were, he and his husband decided to take action. On September 21, 2010, they posted a video on YouTube. They told their experiences from high school, coming out and finding happiness as adults. The message, he said, is simple: it gets better.

He explained his motives in sharing the message in a 2011 interview with National Public Radio.

"I believe when a 13- or 14- or 15-year old gay kid kills himself what he's saying is that he can't picture a future with enough joy to compensate for pain he's in now," he said. "And watching the suicide crisis unfold last fall, my husband and I decided we weren't going to be shamed out of speaking to LGBT youth anymore. And the idea behind the project was for gay adults to talk to queer kids about our lives to give them hope for their futures."

Statistics point to increased danger for the population Savage hoped to reach.

LGBTQ youth are four times more likely as their straight peers to attempt suicide. According to the Trevor Project, a non-profit organization that works to prevent LGBT youth suicide, 90 percent of LGBTQ students were assaulted or harassed during the 2010-2011 school year.

Since Savage's video, more than 30,000 others have provided messages of hope to young people. Videos have been shared by President Barrack Obama and Secretary of State Hillary Clinton, celebrities Tom Hanks and Janet Jackson, Boston Red Sox players and employees of Google and Facebook.

The vast majority of the videos are from average individuals, sharing their stories of overcoming bullying and telling today's youth that "it gets better."

Pierre Phipps of Chicago, a self-described former bully, worked with a friend to create his own video. "The message I was trying to send was that words are really nothing," Phipps said. "Although it may seem like the end of the world, soon you will get over it and be a great person. It gets better."

LeighAnna Dwyer of Boston approached her video differently. Instead of a straightforward message relating her experiences, the 24-year-old shared a piece of performance poetry she created, "Better." She dedicated it to Jamey Rodemeyer, a bisexual New York high school student who created his own "It Gets Better" video, who committed suicide in September 2011 after several years of bullying.

> I want to promise it gets better
> but maybe it stays the same, you just
> learn to Act Up instead of settling down
> raise your head like your pride is a crown and
> you just won
> a beauty pageant
> It doesn't get better, but you do—you get
> a little stronger every day
> and a little less afraid; after you live to realize
> fear isn't the only thing

that makes your heart race:
Love does the same thing…

Fight to keep your
queer heart beating day after day, because if it
stops
you'll never know whether I'm speaking truth
and the one thing I know for certain is there's no
one else in the world
with the same beautiful rhythm
to their pulse
as you.

To learn more about the It Gets Better Project and view the messages, visit itgetsbetter.org [http://www.itgetsbetter.org]. Videos may also be viewed on YouTube by searching "It Gets Better."

— *Dustin Petty*

CPSIA information can be obtained at www.ICGtesting.com
Printed in the USA
LVOW130054170812

294673LV00004B/2/P